The Munro-E Bed and Breakfast Guide

Accommodation for walkers in the Highlands of Scotland

compiled by
Angus Johnson

Prune Publications

First published in Great Britain in 2002 by
Prune Publications, 6 Burns Crescent
Tonbridge, Kent, TN9 2PS
www.munrobaggersb-and-b.co.uk

ISBN 0-9542489-0-2

British Library Cataloguing in Publication Data.
A catalogue record for this book is available from the British Library.

Cover design and illustration,
and maps by Paul Gurney.

*With thanks to: Andrew McManus for his company on
several expeditions (both Munro bagging and B&B hunting);
Nicky Drucquer and Colin Wilkinson for their encouragement
and help – and first class hospitality; Jamie Knott for advice on
presentation and marketing; and last but not least, Martin and
Jill Beard for proof-reading assistance, printing services,
and innumerable cups of coffee.*

*This Guide is dedicated to all the B&B proprietors in the
Highlands, whose excellent hospitality I have enjoyed in the past;
and particularly Mrs Katrine Macleod, formerly of Shieldaig, whose
welcome was an example of Scottish hospitality at its best.*

Printed by ImediaPrint, Centric Close, Oval Road, London NW1

Contents

Introductory ramble.

If you are wondering why this guide is all in black and white, with no pictures, while other guidebooks are in full colour, with pictures, at around the same cost (or even completely free), it's because no B&B proprietor has been charged a penny for having their details included in this guide. This has been done in order to maximise the choice available to you, the reader. In contrast, other guidebooks may charge B&B proprietors considerable sums of money, thereby discouraging many from being included, and therefore reducing the number of places that you have to choose from.

So why another new guidebook? As a keen hillwalker, I couldn't find one that suited my needs and told me what I wanted to know. The ones on offer at the moment seem to include large numbers of entries for tourist hot-spots such as Edinburgh (where I don't want to go), but don't include handy B&Bs that I've found in all sorts of out-of-the-way places. The accommodation entries describe the architecture of the house, the tasteful interior décor, the local tourist attractions, and the stunning scenery (which I'm either not interested in or know about already), but they don't include really important information – such as whether you can have a cooked breakfast at 7am, or whether the proprietors can cope with a pile of wet waterproofs and clothing, or will charge a supplement if you're on your own. So I compiled a guidebook which does do all these things, and thought that perhaps other people would like to have a copy – so here it is.

The geographical grouping of entries roughly follows the order of the sections of Munro's Tables, so if you know which mountains you want to climb, you can find somewhere local. Though the reader should bear in mind that one location can serve as a base for mountains in more than one section. Some cross-references have been included to help in this situation.

As well as accommodation entries, there are suggestions for places to get an evening meal, tea shops, bike hire shops, tourist information offices, and occasional ferry information likely to be of use to the hillwalker. *Please note that times quoted for teas and meals etc. apply to the summer season (unless full year-round information is given) – during the winter it is essential to ring to confirm times and availability.* Recommendations for meals or refreshments added by the compiler are in *italics*.

Notes on accommodation entries.

The layout of each entry is as follows. In the left-hand column:
- contact details, including the postal address with the Post Town in capitals, *which may be some distance from the accommodation described.*
- email address and website if available.
- relevant quality awards; with STB referring to the VisitScotland (previously Scottish Tourist Board) star rating and category. (I have to admit that the rating 'VS ★★★' makes me think of a classic but rather hard rock climb, not a B&B.) If assessed quality is important to you, choose one of these, but there are many excellent quality B&Bs who have decided not to pay the fees for assessment.
- 'Walkers Welcome' indicates membership of the scheme of that name run by VisitScotland.

In the right-hand column:
- the six-figure OS grid reference, preceded by the sheet number of the relevant Landranger 1:50 000 sheet;
- period when open (if a B&B states 'Open all year', the proprietors may close to take a holiday sometime themselves);
- the number of rooms of each type (Single, Twin, Double, Family);
- the cost per night for B&B, and the policy on single occupancy of a twin or double room. If a range of prices is given, this indicates the difference between off-peak and peak season. Please note that single occupancy of a twin/double at no extra charge only applies to genuine single travellers, and not to members of a group who just fancy a room to themselves. *As always, prices quoted are subject to agreement at the time of booking, particularly with regard to single occupancy.*

The remaining details should be self-explanatory, with the following comments:
- The Guide does not attempt to give full details of bathroom facilities. It is assumed, and not stated in each entry, that everywhere will have at least a shower available for the use of guests.
- 'Ensuite avail...' indicates that at least one room has ensuite facilities, and states whether with shower or bath, or with both. '...with shower/bath' indicates that it depends on which room is occupied.
- 'Bath avail.' indicates that, if desired, a bath may be taken instead of a shower, though the availability *may* depend on which room is occupied.
- 'Bath avail. depending on room occ.' indicates that availability *does* depend on the room occupied.
- 'Bath avail. all rooms' means that it does *not* depend on the room occupied, but note that the bath may be a shared one.
- '...by arr.' for breakfast, evening meals, etc, means by prior arrangement; usually taken to mean the evening before for breakfast or packed lunch, or at breakfast for the following evening meal.

- Many proprietors will provide a continental/cold/tray/packed/DIY breakfast if you need it earlier than their stated earliest time.
- 'Day in OK' means that you may stay in your room (or guest lounge, if available) during the day, but this does not apply on your day of arrival or departure, and access to service the room must be allowed at some time.
- 'No smoking' means that smoking is totally banned, if not stated, assume it is restricted and check with the proprietors if you wish to smoke.
- 'Bike storage' means that there is somewhere under cover for your bike, check at the time of booking if you need it to be securely lockable.
- 'Walkers particularly welcome' indicates that the proprietors have rated themselves as making specific efforts to cater for the needs of guests who are walkers; if this is not stated, then walkers are just as much welcome as any other guest.
- 'Book-ahead service' means that the proprietors are willing to make a phone booking for you if you wish to move on to another establishment listed in the Guide; but you should agree the exact terms of the service at the time of request.
- Additional information supplied, or recommendations added by the compiler are in *italics*.

You can help make this guide even better.

Have you found any errors in the information given in the Guide? Do you have any recommendations for more places to be included – B&Bs, places for meals, take-aways, or tea shops? The publishers are always pleased to receive corrections, or suggestions for improvement. We would also value feedback about your experience of staying at places listed in the Guide. Compliments may be published in the Guide; 'points for improvement' may be referred to the relevant proprietor (without any reference to the complainant's name, if this is preferred). Please send details to the compiler at the address given on the back of the title page.

Angus Johnson
Tonbridge

Loch Lomond to Loch Rannoch (Sections 1 & 2)

Balmaha – Tarbet – Arrochar – Comrie – Lochearnhead – Glen Dochart – Crianlarich
Tyndrum – Bridge of Orchy – Killin – Lawers – Fortingall – Kenmore – Aberfeldy

Balmaha *(Stirling)*

Mrs Jenny Cronin
Conic View Cottage, Balmaha
GLASGOW, G63 0JQ
Tel: 01360 870297
email: jenny@conicview.co.uk
web: www.conicview.co.uk
STB ★★★ B&B, Walkers Welcome

56 / NS 421908 Open Mar - Nov. Rooms: 1S, 1T, 1D. S: £20.00 pp T/D: £18.00 pp. Single occ. T/D: off peak only, £12.00 extra. No ensuite. Bath avail. B'fast 7.00am - 8.45am. Packed lunches by arr. Guest lounge. TV in rooms. No smoking. Drying facilities. Bike storage. Walkers particularly welcome. Book-ahead service.

Liz Bates
Bay Cottage, Balmaha
GLASGOW, G63 0JQ
Tel: 01360 870346
email: lizbates@hotmail.com
web: www.visitscotland.com
    /accommodation/index.asp
STB ★★★ B&B, Walkers Welcome

56 / NS 420909 Open Mar - Oct. Rooms: 1S, 1T, 1D, 3F. £21.00 - £23.00 pp. Single occ. T/D: off peak only, £none - £3.00 extra. Ensuite avail. with shower. Bath avail. depending on room occ. B'fast 7.30am - 9.00am, early b'fast by arr. Packed lunches by arr. Eve meal by arr. 7.00pm, £12.50, bring your own drinks. Guest lounge. Day in OK. TV in rooms & guest lounge. No smoking. Drying facilities. Bike storage. Walkers particularly welcome. Book-ahead service. Videos avail. in guest lounge.

Evening/bar meals:
– The Oak Tree Inn, Balmaha, GLASGOW, G63 0JQ 01360 870440   56 / NS 420908
oaktreeinn@btinternet.com www.oaktreeinn.activehotels.com Bar meals all day until 9.30pm.

Tarbet *(Dunbartonshire)*

Mrs E. Fairfield
Lochview, Tarbet
ARROCHAR, G83 7DD
Tel: 01301 702200
email: efairfield@lineone.net
STB ★ B&B

56 / NN 318046 Open all year, except Christmas/N.Year. Rooms: 1S, 1T, 1D, 1F. T/D: £16.00 - £18.00 pp. S: £20.00 pp F: £18.00 pp. Single occ. T/D: off peak only, at single room rate. Ensuite avail. with shower. No bath. B'fast 8.00am - 10.00am, early b'fast from 7.00am by arr. Packed lunches by arr. Guest lounge. Day in OK. TV in guest lounge. Bike storage. Book-ahead service.

Bernadette & John Rainey
Glebe House, Manse Lane
Tarbet, ARROCHAR, G83 7DE
Tel/Fax: 01301 702629
email: Glebe_House@
    hotmail.com
STB ★★★★ B&B

56 / NN 320048 Open all year. Rooms: 1S, 2T, 1D, 1F. S: £22.00 pp T/D: £25.00 pp F: £30.00 per adult, £15.00 per child. Single occ. T/D: off peak only, no extra. Ensuite avail. with shower. Bath avail. B'fast 8.00am - 9.30am, early b'fast from 7.00am by arr. Packed lunches by arr. Eve meal by arr. 6.00pm - 8.00pm, £8.00 - £12.50, bring your own drinks. Guest lounge. Day in OK. TV in rooms & guest lounge. No smoking. Drying facilities. Bike storage. Book ahead service.

Please read the entries in conjunction with the notes on pages 5 & 6.

Malcolm & Marion Brown
Lomondbank House, Tarbet
ARROCHAR, G83 7DG
Tel/Fax: 01301 702258
email: brown-rebus@supanet.com
web: www.stayatlochlomond.com/lomondbank
STB Awaiting Inspection

56 / NN 322049 Open all year. Rooms: 2T, 1D. £25.00 pp. Single occ. T/D: any time, £10.00 extra. Ensuite avail. with shower. Bath avail. B'fast 8.30am, early b'fast from 6.00am by arr. Packed lunches by arr. Guest lounge. TV in rooms. No smoking. Book-ahead service.

Evening/bar meals: see Arrochar
Tourist info: Main Street, Tarbet, ARROCHAR, G83 7DE 01301 702260 (Apr - Oct)

Arrochar (Dunbartonshire)

Bob & Lesley Donnelly
Rowantreebank, Main Street
ARROCHAR, G83 7AA
Tel/Fax: 01301 702318
email: Lesley.Donnelly@
btinternet.com
STB ★★ B&B

56 / NN 298042 Open all year. Rooms: 1S, 1T, 1D, 2F. £17.50 - £22.50 pp.* Single occ. T/D: off peak only, no extra. All rooms ensuite with shower. No bath. B'fast 8.00am - 11.30am, early b'fast from 5.00am by arr. Packed lunches by arr. Eve meal by arr. 7.30pm - 10.00pm, bring your own drinks. Day in room OK. TV in rooms. Drying facilities. Bike storage. Book-ahead service. *Children in family room: £10.00 - £15.00 pp.

Mary & Gordon Chandler
Rowantree Cottage, Main Street
ARROCHAR, G83 7AA
Tel/Fax: 01301 702540
email: rowantreeargyll@aol.com
web: www.arrochar-bb.com
STB ★★★ B&B

56 / NN 298044 Open all year. Rooms: 1T, 1D, 1F. T/D: £22.00 pp F: £18.50 pp. Single occ. T/D: off peak only, £3.00 extra. All rooms ensuite with shower. Bath avail. B'fast 8.00am - 8.30am, early b'fast from 7.30am by arr. Packed lunches by arr. Eve meal by arr. 6.30pm, £12.00, bring your own drinks. Guest lounge. Day in OK. TV in rooms & guest lounge. No smoking. Drying facilities. Bike storage. Book-ahead service.

Ursula & Finlay Craig
Lochside Guest House, Main Street
ARROCHAR, G83 7AA
Tel: 01301 702467
email: LochsideGH@aol.com
web: www.stayatlochlomond.com/lochside
STB ★★★ Guest House

56 / NN 298044 Open all year. Rooms: 1S, 1T, 3D, 1F. S/T/D: £20.00 - £26.00 pp. F: £22.00 - £28.00 pp. Single occ. T/D: any time, 50% extra. Ensuite avail. with shower. Bath avail. B'fast 8.00am - 9.30am, early b'fast from 7.30am by arr. Packed lunches by arr. Residents licence. Guest lounge. Day in OK. TV in rooms & guest lounge. Bike storage. Walkers particularly welcome. Book-ahead service.

Philip & Janet Bagen
Dalkusha House
ARROCHAR, G83 7AA
Tel: 01301 702234 Fax: 01301 702990
email: dalkusha@aol.com
STB ★★★ B&B, Walkers Welcome

56 / NN 298042 Open all year. Rooms: 2T,* 2D. £18.00 - £22.00. Single occ. T/D: any time, £4.00 extra. Ensuite avail. with shower. Bath avail. B'fast 8.30am, early b'fast by arr. Packed lunches by arr. Guest lounge. Day in OK. TV in rooms & guest lounge. No smoking. Drying facilities. Bike storage. Book-ahead service. *One twin room converts to a family room

Prices quoted are subject to agreement at the time of booking, particularly with regard to single occupancy of a twin, double, or family room.

8

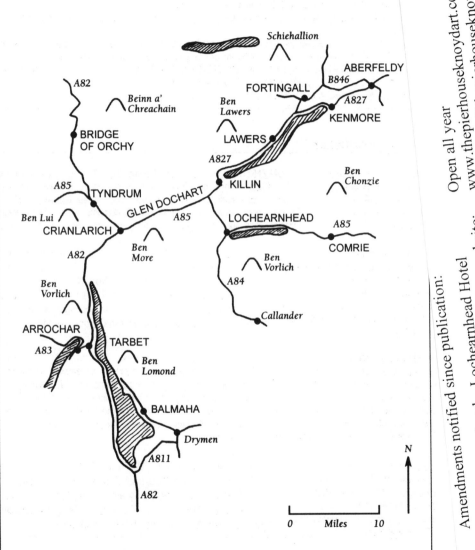

Loch Lomond to Loch Rannoch (Sections 1 & 2)

Schiehallion

A82

Beinn a' Chreachain

Ben Lawers

FORTINGALL

B846

ABERFELDY

A827

KENMORE

BRIDGE OF ORCHY

LAWERS

A827

A85

TYNDRUM

Ben Lui

CRIANLARICH

GLEN DOCHART

A85

KILLIN

Ben Chonzie

LOCHEARNHEAD

A85

COMRIE

A82

Ben More

Ben Vorlich

A84

Ben Vorlich

Callander

ARROCHAR

A83

TARBET

Ben Lomond

BALMAHA

Drymen

A811

A82

N

0   Miles   10

Locations in CAPITALS have listed accommodation

Open all year
www.thepierhouseknoydart.co.uk
stayandeat@thepierhouseknoydart.co.uk

Amendments notified since publication:

Lochearnhead Hotel   new website:
Pier House   new email:

p.11 Lochearnhead
p.42 Inverie

Evening/bar meals:
- Callums Bar, Main Road, ARROCHAR, G83 7AA 01301 702347   56 / NN 298045
  Bar meals all day until 8.00pm.
- The Village Inn, ARROCHAR, G83 7AX 01301 702279   56 / NN 293034
  Bar meals 12.00noon - 5.00pm; *a la carte* restaurant after 5.00pm.
- Loch Long Hotel, ARROCHAR, G83 7AA 01301 702434   56 / NN 299047
  Bar meals 6.00pm - 8.00pm. B&B from around £25.00 pp.
  Excellent food and the best restaurant waiter service I've ever received. Recommended, AJ

Teas etc:
- Craigard Tea Room & Restaurant, Main Road, ARROCHAR, G83 7AA   56 / NN 298046
  01301 702957 Open daily 11.00am - 9.00pm, evening meals Thu - Sun, 6.00pm - 9.00pm.
- Over the Hill Coffee House, Main Road, ARROCHAR, G83 7AA   56 / NN 298042
  01301 702552 Open daily except Mon, 12noon - 10.00pm

Tourist info: Ardgarten, ARROCHAR, G83 7AA 01301 702432 (Apr - Oct)

Comrie *(Perthshire)*

Mr & Mrs L. W. Paterson St Margaret's, Braco Road Comrie, CRIEFF, PH6 2HP Tel: 01764 670413 STB ★★★ B&B	51 / NN 775212 Open Mar - Oct. Rooms: 2T, 1D. T: £18.00 - £20.00 pp D: £18.00 pp. Single occ. T/D: any time, no extra. Ensuite avail. with shower. Bath avail. depending on room occ. B'fast 8.00am - 9.30am. Packed lunches by arr. Day in room OK. TV in rooms. No smoking. Drying facilities. Bike storage. Walkers particularly welcome. Book-ahead service.
Mrs Janet Griffiths Mossgiel Guest House, 5 Burrell Street Comrie, CRIEFF, PH6 2JP Tel/Fax: 01764 670567 email: mossgielcomrie@hotmail.com web: www.mossgielcomrie.freeserve.co.uk AA ◆◆◆	51 / NN 770221 Open Mar - Oct. Rooms: 2T, 1D. £20.00 pp. Single occ. T/D: any time, £5.00 extra. Ensuite avail. with shower. No bath. B'fast 8.00am - 9.00am, early b'fast from 7.30am by arr. Guest lounge. Day in OK. TV in guest lounge. No smoking. Drying facilities. Bike storage. Book-ahead service.
Mrs Madeleine King Vean House, Barrack Road Comrie, CRIEFF, PH6 2EQ Tel: 01764 670869 email: madking1999@btinternet.com web: *under development* STB ★★★ B&B, Walkers Welcome	51 / NN 776216 Open all year. Rooms: 2D. £18.00 pp. Single occ. T/D: any time, no extra. No ensuite. Bath avail. B'fast 8.00am - 9.00am, early b'fast from 7.00am by arr. Packed lunches by arr. Guest lounge. Day in OK. TV in guest lounge. No smoking. Drying facilities. Bike storage. Walkers particularly welcome. Book-ahead service. STB Cyclists Welcome.
Alex & Margaret Coll Langower B&B, Dalginross Comrie, CRIEFF, PH6 2ED Tel: 01764 679990 email: margaretcoll@lineone.net STB ★★★ B&B	51 / NN 774218 Rooms: 1T, 2D. £16.00 - £22.00 pp. Single occ. T/D: any time, £4.00 extra. Ensuite avail. with shower. No bath. B'fast from 7.00am by arr. Packed lunches by arr. Guest lounge. Day in OK. TV in rooms & guest lounge. Drying facilities. Bike storage. Book-ahead service.

It is assumed, and not stated in each entry, that everywhere will have at least a shower available.

– The Earnbank House Hotel, Drummond Street, Comrie, CRIEFF, PH6 2DY   51 / NN 775221
  01764 670239 Bar meals 5.00pm - 9.00pm. B&B from around £27.00 pp.
Bike hire:
– R S Finnie (Cycles), Leadenflower Road, CRIEFF, PH7 3JE 01764 652599

Lochearnhead *(Perthshire)*

Bob & Christine Dunn Briar Cottage LOCHEARNHEAD, FK19 8PU Tel: 01567 830443 email: briarcottbb@aol.com	51 / NN 599239 Open all year. Rooms: 1T, 2D. T: £22.00 pp D: £29.00 pp. Single occ. T/D: any time, £5.00 extra. Ensuite avail. with shower. Bath avail. B'fast 7.00am - 10.00am, early b'fast from 6.00am by arr. Packed lunches by arr. Guest lounge. Day in OK. TV in rooms & guest lounge. Drying facilities. Bike storage. Book-ahead service.
Lochearnhead Hotel LOCHEARNHEAD FK19 8PU Tel: 01567 830229 Fax: 01567 830364 AA ★★	51 / NN 596238 Open Mar - Nov. Rooms: 5T, 4D, 1F. £33.00 pp.* Single occ. T/D: any time, £10.00 extra. Ensuite avail. with shower/bath. Bath avail. depending on room occ. B'fast 8.30am - 9.30am, early b'fast from 7.00am by arr. Packed lunches by arr. Eve meal: dinner 7.00pm - 9.00pm, £19.00; bar meals 5.00pm - 9.30pm. Full licence. Guest lounge. Day in OK. TV in rooms & guest lounge. Drying facilities. Bike storage. Book-ahead service. Rates for DB&B. Off-peak special offers. *Children in family room: half price.
Mrs J Levine Lauriston, Kendrum Road LOCHEARNHEAD FK19 8PX Tel: 01567 830206	51 / NN 589235 Open all year. Rooms: 1S, 1T. £20.00 pp. Single occ. T/D: any time no extra. No ensuite. Bath avail. B'fast 8.00am - 9.00am, early b'fast by arr. Packed lunches by arr. Eve meal by arr. £7.00, bring your own drinks. Guest lounge. Day in OK. TV in guest lounge. No smoking. Drying facilities. Bike storage. Book-ahead service.
Clachan Cottage Hotel Lochside LOCHEARNHEAD, FK19 8PU Tel: 01567 830247 Fax: 01567 830300 web: www.clachancottagehotel. com RAC ★★	51 / NN 596238 Open all year. Rooms: 4S, 8T, 6D, 2F. S: £38.00 pp T/D/F: £28.00 pp. Single occ. T/D: off peak only, £10.00 extra. Ensuite avail. with shower/bath. Bath avail. depending on room occ. B'fast 8.00am - 9.30am, early b'fast from 7.00am by arr. Packed lunches by arr. Eve meals 7.00pm - 9.00pm, set menu £17.50. Full licence. Guest lounge. Day in OK. TV in rooms. Drying facilities. Bike storage. Walkers particularly welcome. Book-ahead service.

Evening/bar meals:
– Lochearnhead Hotel *(see main entry)*
– Clachan Cottage Hotel *(see main entry)*
– The '45' Restaurant & Bar, LOCHEARNHEAD, FK19 8PX 01567 830221   51 / NN 589234
  Bar meals all day until 11.00pm.

'Bath avail.' indicates that, if desired, a bath may be taken instead of a shower, though the availability may depend on which room is occupied.

Glen Dochart (Perthshire)

The Suie Lodge Hotel Glen Dochart CRIANLARICH, FK20 8QT Tel: 01567 820417 Fax: 01567 820040 email: suielodge@btinternet.com STB ★ Small Hotel	51 / NN 488279 Open all year. Rooms: 1S, 4T, 4D, 1F. S: £20.00 - £22.00 pp T/D/F: £22.00 - £25.00 pp. Single occ. T/D: off peak only, £5.00 extra. Ensuite avail. with shower/bath. Bath avail. depending on room occ. B'fast 8.00am - 9.30am, early b'fast from 7.30am by arr. Packed lunches by arr. Meals 11.00am - 9.00pm. Full licence. No guest lounge but seating in lounge area of bar. Day in room OK. TV in rooms. Drying facilities. Bike storage.

Crianlarich (Perthshire)

W. J. C. Christie Inverardran House CRIANLARICH, FK20 8QS Tel: 01838 300240 email: john@inverardran. demon.co.uk web: *under development*	50 / NN 392249 Open all year. Rooms: 1T, 2D. £15.00 - £20.00 pp.* Single occ. T/D: any time, £5.00 extra. No ensuite. Bath avail. B'fast 8.00am - 9.00am, early b'fast from 5.00am by arr. Packed lunches by arr. Evening meal by arr. £5.00 (2 courses), bring your own drinks. Guest lounge. TV in guest lounge. No smoking. Drying facilities. Bike storage. Book-ahead service. *Reduction for longer stays.

I haven't stayed here for a while, but I remember a superb big breakfast. Recommended. AJ.

Maureen & Gordon Gaughan The Lodge House CRIANLARICH, FK20 8RU Tel/Fax: 01838 300276 email: admin@lodgehouse.co.uk web: www.lodgehouse.co.uk STB ★★★★ Guest House Walkers Welcome AA ◆◆◆◆	50 / NN 374260 Open all year, except Christmas. Rooms: 2T, 3D, 1F. From £25.00 pp. Single occ. T/D: any time, £5.00 - £15.00 extra. Ensuite avail. with shower/bath. Bath avail. depending on room occ. B'fast 8.00am - 8.30am, early b'fast from 7.30am by arr. Packed lunches by arr. Eve meal by arr. 7.00pm, £15.00 (4 courses). Residents licence. Guest lounge. TV in rooms. No smoking. Drying facilities. Bike storage. Walkers particularly welcome. Book-ahead service.

Brian Hay & Liz Lawrie Ewich Guest House, Strathfillan CRIANLARICH, FK20 8RU Tel/Fax: 01838 300300 email: enquiries@ewich.co.uk web: www.ewich.co.uk STB ★★★ Guest House Walkers Welcome	50 / NN 362273 Open all year. Rooms: 1S, 3T, 2D. £22.00 - £27.00 pp. Single occ. T/D: any time, £10.00 extra if busy. Ensuite avail. with shower. Bath avail. B'fast 8.00am - 9.00am, early b'fast from 7.00am by arr. Packed lunches by arr. Eve meal by arr. £15.00. Residents licence. Guest lounge. Day in OK. TV in rooms. No smoking. Drying facilities. Bike storage. Walkers particularly welcome. Book-ahead service.

Peter & Carole Flockhart Craigbank Guest House CRIANLARICH FK20 8QS Tel: 01838 300279	50 / NN 387252 Open all year. Rooms: 3T, 1D, 2F. £17.50 pp.* Single occ. T/D: any time, £7.50 extra. Ensuite avail. with shower. No bath. B'fast 8.15am - 8.45am, early b'fast from 7.30am by arr. Packed lunches by arr. Guest lounge. Day in OK. TV in guest lounge. Drying facilities. Bike storage. Book-ahead service. *Children under 12 in family room: £9.00 pp.

Many proprietors will provide a continental/cold/tray/packed/DIY breakfast if you need it earlier than their stated earliest time.

Evening/bar meals:
- Ben More Lodge Hotel, CRIANLARICH, FK20 8QS 01838 300210   50 / NN 390251
  info@ben-more.co.uk www.ben-more.co.uk Nov - Mar open weekends only.
  Bar meals 5.30pm - 8.30pm. B&B from around £33.00 pp.
- Rod & Reel, Main Street, CRIANLARICH, FK20 8QN 01838 300271   50 / NN 386252
  Bar meals all day until 9.30pm.

Teas etc:
- Station Tea Room, CRIANLARICH, F20 8QN 01838 300204   50 / NN 384251
  Open daily, 7.30am - 8.00pm (Apr - Sep); 8.00am - 2.30pm (Oct) Also b'fast, pie & chips, etc.

Tyndrum (Perthshire)

Avril & Harrill Tomkins	50 / NN 329303 Open all year. Rooms: 1S, 3T, 3D, 1F.
Dalkell Cottages, Lower Station Road	S: £25.00 - £28.00 pp T/D: £21.00 - £24.00 pp F: £18.00
Tyndrum, by CRIANLARICH, FK20 8RY	- £21.00 pp. Single occ. T/D: any time, no extra. Ensuite
Tel: 01838 400285 Fax: 01838 400386	avail. with shower/bath. Bath avail. depending on room
Mob: 07771 692129	occ. B'fast 7.45am - 9.30am, early b'fast from 7.30 by arr.
email: htomkins@dalkell.fsnet.co.uk	Packed lunches by arr. Guest lounge. Day in OK. TV in
or: info@dalkell.co.uk	guest lounge. No smoking. Drying facilities. Bike storage.
web: www.dalkell.co.uk	Walkers particularly welcome. Book-ahead service.
STB ★★★ Guest House, Walkers Welcome	

Invervey Hotel, Tyndrum	50 / NN 329305 Open all year. Rooms: 5S, 7T, 6D, 3F. £25.00 pp.
by CRIANLARICH, FK20 8RY	Single occ. T/D: off peak only, no extra. Ensuite avail. with
Tel: 01838 400219	shower/bath. Bath avail. depending on room occ. B'fast 8.00am -
Fax: 01838 400280	11.00am, early b'fast from 7.30am by arr. for groups only. Packed
web: www.inverveyhotel.co.uk	lunches by arr. Eve meals 4.00pm - 10.00pm. Full licence. Guest
STB ★★ Small Hotel	lounge. Day in OK in guest lounge only. TV in rooms & guest lounge.
Walkers Welcome	Drying facilities. Bike storage. Book-ahead service.

I haven't stayed here, but the food and service were both good when I had a meal here. Recommended. AJ

Diane & Jim Mailer	50 / NN 334298 Open all year. Rooms: 1T, 1D, 1F. T/D: £20.00 -
Glengarry House, Tyndrum	£23.00 pp F: £20.00 - £23.00 per adult. Single occ. T/D: off peak
by CRIANLARICH, FK20 8RY	only, £5.00 extra. Ensuite avail. with shower. No bath. B'fast 7.30am
Tel/Fax: 01838 400224	- 9.00am, early b'fast from 7.00am by arr. Packed lunches by arr.
email: glengarry@altavista.net	Eve meal by arr. £12.00, bring your own drinks. Guest lounge. Day
web: www.glengarryhouse.co.uk	in OK. No TV. No smoking. Drying facilities. Bike storage. Walkers
STB ★★★ B&B	particularly welcome. Book-ahead service. Vegetarian meals. Self-
Walkers Welcome	catering chalet avail. sleeps 6. Views of Ben Lui & Ben More.

Evening/bar meals:
- Invervey Hotel *(see main entry)*
- Little Chef, Tyndrum, by CRIANLARICH, FK20 8RY 01838 400235   50 / NN 329304
  Open 7.00am - 10.00pm.

Tourist info: Main Street, Tyndrum, by CRIANLARICH, FK20 8RY 01838 400246 (Apr - Oct)

Please read the entries in conjunction with the notes on pages 5 & 6.

Bridge of Orchy *(Argyll)*

Mrs F. Aitken	50 / NN 322442 Open Apr - Oct. Rooms: 3S, 1T, 1D, 1F. £20.00 pp.
Achallader	Single occ. T/D: any time, no extra. No ensuite. Bath avail. B'fast
BRIDGE OF ORCHY	7.30am - 9.00am, early b'fast from 5.30am by arr. Packed lunches by
PA36 4AG	arr. Eve meal by arr. £10.00, bring your own drinks. Guest lounge. Day
Tel: 01838 400253	in OK. No TV. Drying facilities. Bike storage.

Evening/bar meals:
- Bridge of Orchy Hotel, BRIDGE OF ORCHY, PA36 4AB 01838 400208   50 / NN 297395
  www.bridgeoforchy.co.uk Bar meals 6.00pm - 9.00pm. B&B from around £40.00 pp.

Killin *(Perthshire)*

Mr & Mrs Semple	51 / NN 572327 Open all year. Rooms: 1S, 2T, 3D, 1F.
Drumfinn Guest House	S: £20.00 pp T: £18.00 pp D: £18.00/£20.00 pp F: £18.00 pp.
1 Manse Road, KILLIN, FK21 8UY	Single occ. T/D: off peak only, no extra. Ensuite avail. with
Tel: 01567 820900	shower/bath. Bath avail. depending on room occ. B'fast 7.30am
Fax: 01567 820029	- 9.00am, early b'fast from 7.00am by arr. Packed lunches by
email: drumfinnhouse@beeb.net	arr. Residents licence. Guest lounge. Day in OK. TV in rooms
web: www.altourism.com/uk/drumfinn	& guest lounge. No smoking. Drying facilities. Bike storage.
STB ★★ Guest House	Walkers particularly welcome. Book-ahead service.

Rick & Joan Wells	51 / NN 572328 Open all year. Rooms: 1S, 1T, 3D, 1F. S: £25.00 -
Fairview House, Main Street	£28.00 pp T/D/F: £22.00 - £24.00 pp.* Single occ. T/D: any time,
KILLIN, FK21 8UT	£4.00 - £6.00 extra. Ensuite avail. with shower. Bath avail. by arr.
Tel: 01567 820667	B'fast 8.00am - 8.30am, early b'fast from 7.00am by arr. Packed
email: info@fairview-killin.co.uk	lunches by arr. Eve meal by arr. £15.00, bring your own drinks.
web: www.fairview-killin.co.uk	Guest lounge. Day in OK. TV in guest lounge. No smoking. Drying
STB ★★★ Guest House	facilities. Bike storage. Walkers particularly welcome. Book-ahead
Walkers Welcome	service. *Family room rate depends on age of children.

Evening/bar meals:
- Killin Hotel, Main Street, KILLIN, FK21 8TP 01567 820296   51 / NN 573332
  killinhotel@btinternet.com www.killinhotel.com *A la carte* restaurant.
  B&B from around £29.00 pp.
  Several other places to eat in Killin.

Teas etc:
- Tarmachan Tea Room, KILLIN, FK21 8TN Open daily except Fri,   51 / NN 574331
  mid Mar - 5th Jan, 11.00am - 4.30pm.

Bike hire:
- Killin Outdoor Centre and Mountain Shop, Main Street, KILLIN, FK21 8UJ
  01567 820652 www.killinoutdoor.co.uk

Tourist info: Breadalbane Folklore Centre, Falls of Dochart, KILLIN 01567 820254 (Mar - Nov)

---

*'No smoking' means that smoking is totally banned, if not stated, assume that it is restricted,
and check with the proprietors if you wish to smoke.*

Lawers (Perthshire)

Ben Lawers Hotel, Lawers
by ABERFELDY, PH15 2PA
Tel: 01567 820436
Fax: 01567 820182
email: enquiries@benlawers.
free-online.co.uk

51 / NN 677395 Open all year, but from Oct - Easter open weekends only. Rooms: 1T, 3D. T: £19.00 pp D: £20.00 - £22.50 pp. Single occ. T/D: off peak only, £5.00 extra. Ensuite avail. with shower/bath. Bath avail. B'fast 8.15am - 9.15am, early b'fast from 7.30am by arr. Packed lunches by arr. Eve meals 6.00pm - 9.00pm. Full licence. Day in room OK. TV in rooms. Drying facilities. Bike storage. Book-ahead service.

I haven't stayed here, but I have eaten in the restaurant - the food was excellent. Recommended. AJ

Fortingall (Perthshire)

Mrs Angela Kininmonth
Kinnighallen Farm, Duneaves Road
Fortingall, by ABERFELDY, PH15 2LR
Tel/Fax: 01887 830619
email: a.kininmonth@talk21.com
web: www.heartlander.scotland.net
/home/kinnighallen.htm
STB ★ B&B

51 / NN 756469 Open all year, except Christmas/ N.Year. Rooms: 1S, 1T, 1D. £15.00 - £17.00 pp. Single occ. T/D: any time, no extra. No ensuite. Bath avail. B'fast 8.00am - 9.00am, early b'fast from 7.30am by arr. Day in room OK. TV avail. in hosts lounge. Drying facilities. Bike storage. Walkers particularly welcome. Book-ahead service.

Evening/bar meals:
- Fortingall Hotel, Fortingall, by ABERFELDY, PH15 2NQ 01887 830367   51 / NN 740470
  Bar meals 6.30pm - 9.00pm. B&B from around £35.00 pp.
- Tigh an Loan Hotel, Fearnan, by ABERFELDY, PH15 2PF 01887 830249   51 / NN 720444
  Bar meals 6.00pm - 9.00pm. B&B from around £31.00 pp.

Kenmore (Perthshire)

Jane & Hamish Fraser
Tigh na Cladiach, Pier Road
Kenmore
by ABERFELDY, PH15 2HG
Tel: 01887 830206
email: janefraser100@aol.com

51 / NN 771454 Open all year. Rooms: 1T. £21.00 pp. Single occ. T/D: off peak only, £none - £5.00 extra. Room ensuite with shower & bath. B'fast 8.00am - 9.00am, early b'fast by arr. Packed lunches by arr. Day in room OK by arr. TV in room. No smoking. Limited drying facilities. Limited bike storage. Book-ahead service.

Evening/bar meals:
- Kenmore Hotel, The Square, Kenmore, by ABERFELDY, PH15 2NU   51 / NN 773455
  01887 830205 reception@kenmorehotel.co.uk www.kenmorehotel.com
  A la carte restaurant. B&B from around £42.00 pp.

Teas etc:
- Taymouth Trading Co, Pier Road, Kenmore, by ABERFELDY, PH15 2HG   51 / NN 771454
  01887 830285 Open daily, Mar - Nov, 10.00am - 5.30pm.

Bike hire:
- Perthshire Mountain Bikes, Pier Road, Kenmore, by ABERFELDY, PH15 2HG
  01887 830291 www.loch-tay.co.uk

15

Aberfeldy (Perthshire)

Kate & George Scott
Tighnabruaich, Taybridge Terrace
ABERFELDY, PH15 2BS
Tel: 01887 820456
Fax: 01887 829254
email: katesscott123@aol.com
STB ★★★ B&B, Walkers Welcome

52 / NN 853492 Open Apr - Oct. Rooms: 2S, 1T. £18.00 - £20.00 pp. Single occ. T/D: any time, no extra. No ensuite. Bath avail. B'fast any time, early b'fast from 6.00am by arr. Packed lunches by arr. Guest lounge. Day in OK. TV in guest lounge. No smoking. Drying facilities. Bike storage. Walkers particularly welcome. Book-ahead service. Snack avail. if arriving late.

Eric & Audrey Slorance
Claremont, Taybridge Road
ABERFELDY, PH15 2BH
Tel: 01887 829370 Fax: 01887 829358
email: Slorance@aberfeldy.fsbusiness.co.uk
STB ★★★ B&B

52 / NN 853491 Open Feb - Nov. Rooms: 1T, 1D, 1F. £18.00 - £22.00 pp. Single occ. T/D: any time, no extra. No ensuite. Bath avail. B'fast 8.30am - 9.00am, early b'fast from 7.00am by arr. Packed lunches by arr. Day in room OK. TV in rooms. No smoking. Bike storage.

Marjorie Ross
Ardtornish, Kenmore Street
ABERFELDY, PH15 2BL
Tel: 01887 820629
email: ardtornish@talk21.com
STB ★★★ B&B

52 / NN 853490 Open all year, except Christmas/N.Year. Rooms: 1T, 1D, 1F. T/F: £18.00 pp D: £20.00 pp. Single occ. T/D: off peak only, no extra. Ensuite avail. with shower. Bath avail. depending on room occ. B'fast 8.00am - 9.00am, early b'fast by arr. Packed lunches by arr. Guest lounge. TV in some rooms. No smoking. Drying facilities. Limited bike storage. Book-ahead service.

Evening/bar meals: plenty of choice in Aberfeldy.
Tourist info: The Square, ABERFELDY, PH15 2DD 01887 820276 (All year)

Loch Etive to Loch Leven (Section 3)

Connel – Taynuilt – Dalmally – Glencoe – Ballachulish
For south-eastern mountains see also Tyndrum and Bridge of Orchy (Sections 1&2)
For northern mountains see also Kinlochleven, North Ballachulish and Onich (Section 4)

Connel (Argyll)

Dunstaffnage Arms Hotel Connel, by OBAN PA37 1PJ Tel: 01631 710666 email: sallyd@supanet.com STB ★★ Small Hotel	49 / NM 909342 Open all year. Rooms: 1S, 2T, 3D, 1F. £20.00 - £25.00 pp. Single occ. T/D: any time, £5.00 - £10.00 extra. Ensuite avail. with shower/bath. Bath avail. depending on room occ. B'fast 8.00am - 9.00am.* Packed lunches by arr. Eve meals 5.30pm - 8.30pm. Full licence. Guest lounge. Day in OK. TV in rooms. Limited drying facilities. Bike storage. Book-ahead service. *Continental b'fast avail. earlier by arr.
Mrs Maclean Greenacre Guest House Connel, by OBAN PA37 1PJ Tel: 01631 710756 STB ★★ Guest House	49 / NM 908341 Open all year. Rooms: 1T, 2D, 2F. £15.00 - £20.00 pp. Single occ. T/D: off peak only, £5.00 extra. Ensuite avail. with shower. No bath. B'fast 8.30am - 9.00am, early b'fast any time by arr. Packed lunches by arr. Eve meal by arr. 7.00pm - 9.00pm, £15.00, bring your own drinks. Guest lounge. Day in OK. TV in rooms & guest lounge. Drying facilities. Bike storage. Walkers particularly welcome. Book-ahead service.

Evening/bar meals:
– Dunstaffnage Arms Hotel *(see main entry)*
Bike hire:
– Oban Cycles, 29 Lochside Street, OBAN, PA34 4HP 01631 566996

Taynuilt (Argyll)

Mrs Wilson Fasnakyle TAYNUILT, PA35 1JN Tel: 01866 822312	50 / NN 003311 Open all year. Rooms: 1S, 1T, 1D. £15.00 pp. Single occ. T/D: any time, no extra. No ensuite. Bath avail. B'fast 7.00am - 10.00am, early b'fast from 6.00am by arr. Packed lunches by arr. Guest lounge. Day in OK. TV in guest lounge. Drying facilities. Bike storage. Walkers particularly welcome. Book-ahead service.
The Taynuilt Hotel TAYNUILT, PA35 1JN Tel: 01866 822437 email: enquiries@ taynuilthotel.co.uk web: www.taynuilthotel.co.uk	50 / NN 003310 Open all year. Rooms: 2S, 4T, 5D, 1F. S: £22.50 pp T/D: £25.00 pp F: £65.00 per room. Single occ. T/D: any time, £10.00 extra. All rooms ensuite with shower/bath. Bath avail. depending on room occ. B'fast 8.00am - 9.00am.* Packed lunch by arr. Eve meals 6.00pm - 9.30pm. Full licence. Guest lounge. Day in OK. TV in rooms. Drying facilities. Bike storage. Book-ahead service. *Cold b'fast avail. earlier.

Evening/bar meals:
– The Taynuilt Hotel *(see main entry)*
Teas etc:
– Robins Nest Tearoom, Main Street, TAYNUILT, PA35 1JE 01866 822429   50 / NN 004312
  Open daily, 10.00am - 5.00pm (Easter - Oct); open Thurs - Sun 10.00am - 4.30pm (Winter).
  Homebaking, snack lunches.

Dalmally (Argyll)

Sandra & Tim Boardman
Craigroyston
DALMALLY, PA33 1AA
Tel: 01838 200234
email: bandb@craigroyston.com
web: www.craigroyston.com
STB ★★★ B&B

50 / NN 158271 Open all year. Rooms: 1S, 1T, 1D. S/T: £17.00 pp D: £18.00 pp. Single occ. T/D: any time, no extra. Ensuite avail. with shower. Bath avail. B'fast 8.00am - 10.00am, early b'fast from 6.00am by arr. Packed lunches by arr. Eve meal by arr. 6.00pm - 8.00pm, £11.00 (3 courses), bring your own drinks. Guest lounge. Day in OK. TV in rooms. No smoking. Drying facilities. Bike storage. Walkers particularly welcome. Book-ahead service. Reduction 3 nights.

Margaret & Tony Cressey
Craig Villa Guest House
DALMALLY, PA33 1AX
Tel/Fax: 01838 200255
email: tonycressey@
craigvilla.co.uk
web: www.craigvilla.co.uk
STB ★★★ B&B
Walkers Welcome

50 / NN 168272 Open all year, except Christmas/N.Year. Rooms: 2T, 2D, 2F. £20.00 - £23.00 pp.* Single occ. T/D: off peak only, £5.00 - £7.00 extra. Ensuite avail. with shower/bath. Bath avail. depending on room occ. B'fast 8.00am - 8.30am, early b'fast from 7.30am by arr. Packed lunches by arr. Eve meal by arr. 7.00pm, £12.50 - £13.00 (4 courses), bring your own drinks. Guest lounge. Day in OK. TV in guest lounge. Drying facilities. Bike storage. Walkers particularly welcome. Book-ahead service. *Children's rates apply in family room.

Jinty & John Burke
Orchy Bank Guest House
DALMALLY, PA33 1AS
Tel: 01838 200370
email: aj.burke@talk21.com
web: www.loch-awe.com/orchybank
STB ★★ Guest House
Walkers Welcome

50 / NN 165276 Open all year, except Christmas/N.Year. Rooms: 2S, 2T, 1D, 2F. £18.00 pp.* Single occ. T/D: any time, £10.00 extra. No ensuite. Bath (2) avail. all rooms. B'fast 7.30am - 8.30am, early b'fast from 6.00am by arr. Packed lunches by arr. Guest lounge. Day in OK. TV in guest lounge. Drying facilities. Bike storage. Walkers particularly welcome. Book-ahead service. *Children under 11 in family room: half price.

Mike & Maureen Borrett
Cruachan Guest House
DALMALLY, PA33 1AA
Tel: 01838 200496
Fax: 01838 200650
email: mborrett@onetel.net.uk
web: www.cruachan-
dalmally.co.uk
STB ★★★ B&B

50 / NN 158271 Open all year. Rooms: 1T, 2D.* £17.50 - £20.00 pp. Single occ. T/D: off peak only, £5.00 extra. Ensuite avail. with shower. Bath avail. depending on room occ. B'fast 7.30am - 9.00am, early b'fast from 7.00am by arr. Packed lunches by arr. Eve meal by arr. 6.00pm - 8.00pm, £10.00 (2 courses) £15.00 (3 courses + wine), bring your own drinks. Guest lounge. Day in OK. TV in rooms. No smoking. Drying facilities. Bike storage. Walkers particularly welcome. Book-ahead service. *One double converts to family room, with third person at: £12.50 - £20.00 pp. Fresh local produce used in meals.

Mrs Morag MacDougall
Strathorchy
DALMALLY, PA33 1AE
Tel/Fax: 01838 200373
email: strathorchy@loch-awe.com
web: www.loch-awe.com/strathorchy
STB ★★★ B&B, Walkers Welcome

50 / NN 144276 Open all year, except 24th, 25th, 31st Dec. Rooms: 1T, 2D. £17.00 - £20.00 pp. Single occ. T/D: any time, no extra. Ensuite avail. with shower/bath. Bath avail. B'fast 7.30am - 9.30am, early b'fast from 7.00am by arr. Packed lunches by arr. Guest lounge. Day in OK. TV in rooms & guest lounge. Drying facilities. Bike storage. Book-ahead service.

Evening/bar meals:
- Glenorchy Lodge Hotel, DALMALLY, PA33 1AA 01838 200312   50 / NN 164272
  hotel@glenorchylodge.freeserve.co.uk www.glenorchylodgehotel.co.uk Bar meals 5.00pm - 9.00pm (Mon - Fri), all day until 9.00pm (Sat, Sun). B&B from around £25.00 pp.

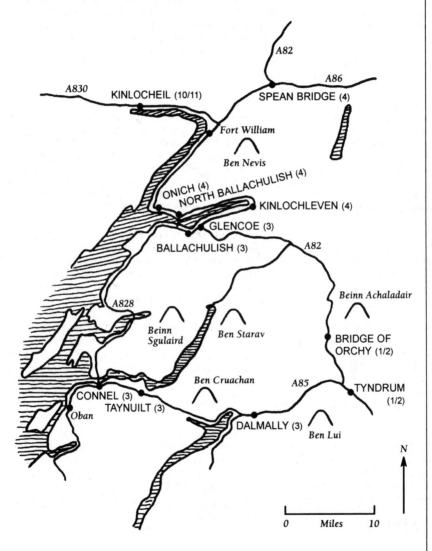

Loch Etive to Loch Treig (Section 3, Section 4)

A82

A86

A830

KINLOCHEIL (10/11)

SPEAN BRIDGE (4)

Fort William

Ben Nevis

ONICH (4) NORTH BALLACHULISH (4)

KINLOCHLEVEN (4)

GLENCOE (3)

BALLACHULISH (3)

A82

Beinn Achaladair

A828

Beinn Sgulaird

Ben Starav

BRIDGE OF ORCHY (1/2)

Ben Cruachan

A85

TYNDRUM (1/2)

CONNEL (3)
TAYNUILT (3)

Oban

DALMALLY (3)

Ben Lui

N

0   Miles   10

Locations in CAPITALS have listed accommodation

Glencoe (Argyll)

Clachaig Inn
Glencoe, BALLACHULISH
PH49 4HX
Tel: 01855 811252
Fax: 01855 811679
email: info@clachaig.com
web: www.clachaig.com
STB ★★ Inn, Walkers Welcome

41 / NN 127567 Open all year. Rooms: 2S, 6T, 8D, 4F. S: £26.00 - £32.00 pp T: £26.00 - £38.00 pp D: £22.00 - £38.00 pp F: £28.00 - £36.00 per adult. Single occ. T/D: off peak occasionally, £varies extra. Ensuite avail. with shower/bath. Bath avail. depending on room occ. B'fast 8.30am - 9.30am.* Packed lunches by arr. Meals 12.00noon - 9.00pm. Full licence. Day in room OK. TV in rooms. Drying facilities. Bike storage. Walkers particularly welcome. *Cold b'fast tray avail. earlier by arr. Self-catering lodges also avail.

The classic walkers and climbers inn – good food, good beer, wide range of single malts, and one of the best locations in the Highlands. Recommended. AJ

Graham & Joyce Hayden
Dorrington Lodge Guest House
Tigh-Phuirt, Glencoe
BALLACHULISH, PH49 4HN
Tel: 01855 811653 Fax: 01855 811995
email: info@dorrington-lodge.com
web: www.dorrington-lodge.com
STB ★★★ Guest House
Walkers Welcome

41 / NN 092585 Open all year, except Christmas/N.Year. Rooms: 2T, 2D. £18.00 - £22.00 pp. Single occ T/D: any time, £2.00 - £5.00 extra.* Ensuite avail. with shower. No bath. B'fast 8.00am - 9.00am, early b'fast from 7.30am by arr. Packed lunches by arr. Eve meal by arr. 7.00pm, £10.00 (2 courses) - £15.00 (3 courses), bring your own drinks. Guest lounge. Day in OK. TV in rooms. No smoking. Drying room. Bike storage. Walkers particularly welcome. Book-ahead service. *Only one room avail. for single occ.

Lynn & Geoff Allman
Callart View, Invercoe, Glencoe
BALLACHULISH, PH49 4HP
Tel: 01855 811259
email: callartview@hotmail.com
web: www.callartview.co.uk

41 / NN 099595 Open all year. Rooms: 1T, 1D. £17.00 - £22.00 pp. Single occ. T/D: any time, £2.00 extra. Ensuite avail. with shower. Bath avail. B'fast 8.00am - 9.00am, early b'fast from 6.00am by arr. Packed lunches by arr. Day in room OK. TV in rooms. No smoking. Drying facilities. Bike storage. Walkers particularly welcome. Book-ahead service. Hillwalking proprietors.

Sally & John Mortimer
Scorrybreac Guest House, Glencoe
BALLACHULISH, PH49 4HT
Tel/Fax: 01855 811354
email: info@scorrybreac.fsnet.co.uk
web: www.scorrybreac.co.uk
STB ★★★ Guest House AA ◆◆◆

41 / NN 103592 Open 26th Dec - 31st Oct. Rooms: 3T, 3D. £18.00 - £25.00 pp. Single occ. T/D: any time, £2.00 - £15.00 extra. Ensuite avail. with shower. No bath. B'fast 8.00am - 8.30am. Guest lounge. TV in rooms. No smoking. Drying facilities. Bike storage. Walkers particularly welcome. Book-ahead service.

Mrs K. Rodger
An Darag, Upper Carnoch, Glencoe
BALLACHULISH, PH49 4HU
Tel: 01855 811643
email: karin.rodger@virgin.net
web: www.visitscotland.com
/accommodation/index.asp
STB ★★★ B&B

41 / NN 105585 Open all year. Rooms: 1T, 1D, 1F. £16.00 - £19.00 pp. Single occ. T/D: off peak only, no extra. Ensuite avail. with shower. No bath. B'fast 8.00am - 9.00am, early b'fast from 7.00am by arr. Packed lunches by arr. Guest lounge. Day in OK. TV in rooms & guest lounge. No smoking. Bike storage. Walkers particularly welcome. Book-ahead service.

'Bath avail. depending on room occ.' indicates that a bath may be taken instead of a shower, but whether this is available depends on which room is occupied.

Mrs Eileen Daynes
Strathlachlan – The Glencoe Guest House
Upper Carnoch, Glencoe
BALLACHULISH, PH49 4HU
Tel: 01855 811244 Fax 01855 811873
email: guesthouse@glencoe-scotland.co.uk
or: info@glencoeguesthouse.com
web: www.glencoeguesthouse.com
STB ★★★ Guest House

41 / NN 106585 Open all year, except Christmas. Rooms: 1S, 3T, 3D, 1F. S: £20.00 - £25.00 pp T/D/F: £18.00 - £25.00 pp. Single occ. T/D: off peak only, £2.00 - £5.00 extra. Ensuite avail. with shower/bath. Bath avail. depending on room occ. B'fast 8.00am - 9.00am, early b'fast from 7.30am by arr. Packed lunches by arr. Guest lounge. Day in OK. TV in rooms & guest lounge. No smoking. Drying facilities. Walkers particularly welcome. Book-ahead service.

Evening/bar meals:
- Clachaig Inn *(see main entry)*
- Kings House Hotel, Glencoe, BALLACHULISH, PH49 4HY 01855 851259   41 / NN 259546
  www.kingy.com Bar meals 12noon - 8.30pm. B&B from around £30.00 pp.
- Glencoe Hotel, Glencoe, BALLACHULISH, PH49 4HW 01855 811245   41 / NN 098586
  Bar meals 6.00pm - 9.00pm. B&B from around £30.00 pp.

Teas etc:
- Mrs Matheson's Tea Room & Restaurant, 9 Lorne Drive, Glencoe,   41 / NN 100588
  BALLACHULISH, PH49 4HR 01855 811590 Anne.Matheson@btinternet.com
  www.mrsmathesons-glencoe.com Open daily, Easter - mid Oct, 11.00am - 9.00pm.
  Evening meals from 6.00pm.

Ballachulish *(Argyll)*

Mrs Diana MacAskill
Parkview, 18 Park Road
BALLACHULISH, PH49 4JS
Tel: 01855 811560
email: db.macaskill@talk21.com
web: www.glencoe-parkview.co.uk
STB ★★★ B&B, Walkers Welcome
Friendly welcome and a good breakfast. Recommended. AJ

41 / NN 081582 Open all year, except Christmas. Rooms: 1S, 1T, 2D. S: £20.00 pp T/D: £16.00 - £20.00 pp. Single occ. T/D: off peak only, £2.00 extra. No ensuite. Bath avail. B'fast 8.00am - 8.30am, early b'fast by arr. Packed lunches by arr. Guest lounge. Day in OK. TV in guest lounge. Drying facilities. Bike storage. Walkers particularly welcome. Book-ahead service off-peak season only.

Graham & Gillian Castles
Inverlaroch, Albert Road
BALLACHULISH, PH49 4JR
Tel: 01855 811726
email: grahamt@inverlaroch.fsnet.co.uk
web: www.scotland2000.com/inverlaroch

41 / NN 080583 Open all year, except Christmas/N.Year. Rooms: 1T, 1D, 1F. £19.00 pp. No single occ. T/D. Ensuite avail. with shower. No bath. B'fast 8.30am, early b'fast from 8.00am by arr. Guest lounge. TV in rooms. No smoking. Bike storage. Book-ahead service. 3 nights stay £50.00 pp.

Ken & June Chandler
Fern Villa Guest House, Loan Fern
BALLACHULISH, PH49 4JE
Tel: 01855 811393 Fax: 01855 811727
email: mb@fernvilla.com
web: www.fernvilla.com
STB ★★★ Guest House
Walkers Welcome AA ◆◆◆◆

41 / NN 082581 Open all year. Rooms: 2T, 3D. £21.00 - £23.00 pp. No single occ. T/D. Ensuite avail. with shower. Bath avail. depending on room occ. B'fast 8.30am, early b'fast by arr. Packed lunches by arr. Eve meal by arr. 7.00pm, £12.00. Residents licence. Guest lounge. Day in OK. TV in rooms & guest lounge. No smoking. Drying facilities. Bike storage. Walkers particularly welcome. Book-ahead service.

Lynn & John Bowen
Strathassynt Guest House, Loan Fern
BALLACHULISH, PH49 4JB
Tel: 01855 811261 Fax: 01855 811914
email: info@strathassynt.com
or: res@strathassynt.demon.co.uk
web: www.strathassynt.com
STB ★★★ Guest House
Walkers Welcome

41 / NN 083583 Open all year. Rooms: 1S, 2T, 3D, 1F. S: £20.00 - £28.00 pp T/D: £18.00 - £23.00 pp F: £54.00 - £69.00 per room (2 adults + 2 children). Single occ. T/D: any time, £5.00 extra. Ensuite avail. with shower. No bath. B'fast 8.00am - 9.00am, early b'fast from 7.00am by arr. Packed lunches by arr. Eve meal by arr. 6.00pm - 8.00pm, £10.00 - £13.00. Residents licence. Guest lounge. Day in OK. TV in rooms. No smoking. Drying facilities. Bike storage. Walkers particularly welcome. Book-ahead service.

Mrs Jeanette Watt
Riverside House, Loan Fern
BALLACHULISH
PH49 4JE
Tel: 01855 811473
STB ★★★ B&B

41 / NN 081581 Open Easter - Oct. Rooms: 1T, 2D. £18.00 - £20.00 pp. Single occ. T/D: off peak only, £5.00 extra. Ensuite avail. with shower. Bath avail. depending on room occ. B'fast 7.30am - 9.00am, early b'fast from 6.30am by arr. Packed lunches by arr. Guest lounge. Day in OK. TV in guest lounge. No smoking. Drying facilities. Bike storage. Book-ahead service.

John & Priscilla MacLeod
Lyn Leven Guest House, West Laroch
BALLACHULISH, PH49 4JP
Tel: 01855 811392 Fax: 01855 811600
email: lynleven@amserve.net
web: www.lynleven.co.uk
STB ★★★★ Guest House
AA ◆◆◆◆ RAC ◆◆◆◆

41 / NN 077582 Open all year, except Christmas. Rooms: 1S, 5T, 3D, 3F. S: £29.00 pp T/D: £24.00 pp F: £66.00 per room. Single occ. T/D: any time, £5.00 extra. Ensuite avail. with shower/bath. Bath avail. B'fast 8.00am - 9.00am, early b'fast from 7.30am by arr. Packed lunches by arr. Eve meal by arr. 7.00pm - 8.00pm, £9.00. Residents licence. Guest lounge. Day in OK. TV in rooms & guest lounge. Drying facilities. Bike storage. Walkers particularly welcome. Book-ahead service.

Roselyn Harries
Cuildaff, School Road
West Laroch
BALLACHULISH, PH49 4JQ
Tel: 01855 811436
email: roselyn.harries@
        talk21.com
STB ★★ B&B

41 / NN 080579 Open all year. Rooms: 1S, 1T, 2D. S: £18.00 pp T: £16.00 - £17.00 pp D: £16.00 - £18.00 pp. Single occ. T/D: any time, £5.00 - £10.00 extra. Ensuite avail. with shower. Bath avail. depending on room occ. B'fast 7.30am - 10.30am, early b'fast from 7.00am by arr. Packed lunches by arr. Eve meal by arr. winter only, 6.00pm - 8.00pm, £6.00 - £7.50, bring your own drinks. Day in room OK. TV in rooms. Drying facilities. Bike storage. Walkers particularly welcome. Book-ahead service.

Evening/bar meals:
– The Laroch Lounge Bar, Albert Road, BALLACHULISH,   41 / NN 083583
    01855 811700 Bar meals 5.30pm - 9.00pm. *Good food. Recommended. AJ*
Tourist info: BALLACHULISH, PH49 4JB 01855 811296 (Apr - Oct)

Loch Leven to Loch Treig (Section 4)

Kinlochleven – North Ballachulish – Onich – Spean Bridge
For north-eastern mountains see also Dalwhinnie, Laggan Bridge and Newtonmore
(Sections 5&9)
For southern mountains see also Glencoe and Ballachulish (Section 3)

Kinlochleven *(Argyll)*

Miss C. MacAngus Hermon, Rob Roy Road KINLOCHLEVEN, PH50 4RA Tel: 01855 831383 email: h.macangus@ tinyworld.co.uk	41 / NN 190622 Open Easter - Oct. Rooms: 2T, 1D. £18.00 pp. Single occ. T/D: any time, £7.00 extra. Ensuite avail. with shower. Bath avail. B'fast 7.30am - 9.00am, early b'fast from 7.00am by arr. Packed lunches by arr. Guest lounge. Day in OK. TV in guest lounge. No smoking. Drying facilities. Bike storage. Walkers particularly welcome. Book-ahead service.
Mrs Marion Sweeney Failte, 6 Lovat Road KINLOCHLEVEN, PH50 4RQ Tel: 01855 831394 STB ★★ B&B, Walkers Welcome	41 / NN 191621 Open Easter - Oct. Rooms: 2T. £17.00 pp. Single occ. T/D: any time, £8.00 extra. No ensuite. Bath avail. B'fast 6.30am - 9.30am, early b'fast from 6.00am by arr. Packed lunches by arr. Day in room OK. TV in rooms. Drying facilities. Book-ahead service.
Elsie & Drew Robertson Edencoille, Garbhein Road KINLOCHLEVEN, PH50 4SE Tel/Fax: 01855 831358 STB ★★★ B&B Walkers Welcome	41 / NN 182618 Open all year. Rooms: 2T, 1D, 2F. £18.00 - £22.00 pp. Single occ. T/D: any time, £10.00 extra. Ensuite avail. with shower. Bath avail. B'fast 7.00am - 9.00am, early b'fast by arr. Packed lunches by arr. Eve meal by arr. 6.00pm - 9.00pm, £12.00, bring your own drinks. Guest lounge. Day in OK. TV in rooms & guest lounge. Drying facilities. Bike storage. Walkers particularly welcome. Book-ahead service.

Evening/bar meals:
- Macdonald Hotel, Fort William Road, KINLOCHLEVEN, PH50 4QL   41 / NN 182622
  01855 831539 enquiries@macdonaldhotel.demon.co.uk www.macdonaldhotel.co.uk
  Bar meals 6.00pm - 8.45pm. B&B from around £30.00 pp.
- The Tailrace Inn, Riverside Road, KINLOCHLEVEN, PH50 4QH   41 / NN 187620
  01855 831777 tailrace@btconnect.com www.tailraceinn.co.uk
  Bar meals all day until 8.00pm. B&B from around £24.00 pp.

North Ballachulish *(Inverness-shire)*

Mrs Margaret Banks Brudair, Bail Ur, North Ballachulish Onich, FORT WILLIAM, PH33 6SB Tel: 01855 821431 email: phillip@henbanks.freeserve.co.uk web: www.henbanks.freeserve.co.uk STB ★★★ B&B, Walkers Welcome	41 / NN 054603 Open all year. Rooms: 2T, 1D. £17.00 pp. Single occ. T/D: any time, £5.00 extra. No ensuite. Bath avail. B'fast 7.30am - 8.30am, early b'fast from 6.30am by arr. Packed lunches by arr. Eve meal by arr. 6.00pm - 8.00pm, bring your own drinks. Guest lounge. Day in OK. TV in rooms & guest lounge. No smoking. Drying facilities. Bike storage. Book-ahead service.

Evening/bar meals: see also Onich

Onich *(Inverness-shire)*

Ronald & Helen Young
Camus House Lochside Guest House
Onich, by FORT WILLIAM, PH33 6RY
Tel/Fax: 01855 821200
email: young@camushouse.freeserve.co.uk
web: www.smoothhound.co.uk
/hotels/camushouse
STB ★★★ Guest House

41 / NN 030614 Open Feb - Nov & N.Year. Rooms: 2T, 3D, 2F. T/D: £26.00 - £30.00 pp F: £60.00 - £80.00 per room. Single occ. T/D: off peak only, £6.00 extra. Ensuite avail. with shower/bath. Bath avail. depending on room occ. B'fast 8.15am - 9.00am. Packed lunches by arr. Residents licence. Guest lounge. Day in OK. TV in rooms & guest lounge. Drying facilities. Bike storage. Walkers particularly welcome. Book-ahead service.

Mrs A. MacKinnon
Highland Croft, 8 Onich
by FORT WILLIAM
PH33 6SD
Tel: 01855 821308
email: annabel_mackinnon@
thefreeinternet.com

41 / NN 027614 Open May - Sep. Rooms: 2T, 2D. £16.00 - £20.00 pp. Single occ. T/D: any time, no extra. Ensuite avail. with shower/bath. Bath avail. B'fast 8.00am - 9.00am, early b'fast from 6.00am by arr. Packed lunches by arr. Eve meal by arr. 6.00pm - 7.30pm, £9.00, bring your own drinks. Guest lounge. TV in guest lounge. No smoking. Drying facilities. Bike storage. Book-ahead service.

Mary Michie
Old Manse, Onich
by FORT WILLIAM, PH33 6RY
Tel: 01855 821202
Fax: 01855 821312
email: oldmanse.onich@
btinternet.com
web: www.onich.co.uk
STB ★★★ B&B

41 / NN 032614 Open Easter - Oct. Rooms: 1D, 1F. D: £15.00 - £20.00 pp F: £18.00 - £22.00 pp.* Single occ. T/D: any time, £10.00 - £12.00 extra. Ensuite avail. with shower. Bath avail. depending on room occ. B'fast** 7.30am - 9.00am, early b'fast any time by arr. Packed lunches by arr. Guest lounge. Day in OK. TV in rooms. No smoking. Bike storage. Book-ahead service. *Children in family room: £8.00 - £12.00 pp. **Continental b'fast only. Guests have free use of leisure centre at Isles of Glencoe Hotel, incl. jacuzzi, sauna, pool, mini-gym; also 25% discount on meals at the hotel bistro.

Mrs E. Redfern
Glencairn, Onich
by FORT WILLIAM
PH33 6RY
Tel: 01855 821209

41 / NN 045611 Open all year. Rooms: 1S, 1T, 2D, 1F. S/T/D: £15.00 - £16.00 pp F: £40.00 per room. Single occ. T/D: off peak only, no extra. No ensuite. Bath avail. B'fast 8.30am. Guest lounge. Day in OK. TV in guest lounge. Drying facilities. Bike storage. Book-ahead service.

Mrs K. A. MacCallum
Tigh-a-Righ Guest House
Onich
by FORT WILLIAM
PH33 6SE
Tel: 01855 821255
STB ★★ Guest House

41 / NN 025628 Open all year. Rooms: 2T, 2D*, 2F. £16.00 - £18.00 pp. Single occ. T/D: any time, no extra. Ensuite avail. with shower. Bath avail. all rooms. B'fast 8.00am - 9.15am, early b'fast by arr. Packed lunches by arr. Eve meal by arr. 6.30pm - 8.30pm, £10.00 (3 courses), bring your own drinks. Guest lounges (smoking/non-smoking). Day in OK. TV in rooms. Drying facilities. Bike storage by arr. Walkers particularly welcome. Book-ahead service. *One double converts to twin. Self-catering avail. sleeps up to 12.

Evening/bar meals:
- Onich Hotel, Onich, by FORT WILLAM, PH33 6RY 01855 821214   41 / NN 032613
  reservations@onich-fortwilliam.co.uk www.onich-fortwilliam.co.uk
  Bar meals 12noon - 9.00pm. B&B from around £50.00 pp.
- Creag Mhor Hotel, Onich, by FORT WILLIAM, PH33 6RY 01855 821379   41 / NN 046611
  creagmhor.hotel@virgin.net Bar meals 12noon - 9.00pm. B&B from around £30.00 pp.

Spean Bridge (Inverness-shire)

Mike & Kate Jenkinson
The Braes Guest House, Tirindrish
SPEAN BRIDGE, PH34 4EU
Tel: 01397 712437
Fax: 01397 712108
email: enquiry@thebraes.co.uk
web: www.thebraes.co.uk
STB ★★★ Guest House
Walkers Welcome

41 / NN 231820 Open all year. Rooms: 1S, 1T, 5D. £20.00 - £26.00 pp. Single occ. T/D: any time, £none - £10.00 extra. Ensuite avail. with shower. Bath avail. depending on room occ. B'fast 8.30am - 9.00am, early b'fast from 6.00am by arr. Packed lunches by arr. Eve meal by arr. 5.00pm - 8.30pm, £7.00 (2 courses) - £14.00 (5 courses), bring your own drinks. Guest lounge. Day in OK. TV in guest lounge. No smoking. Drying facilities. Bike storage. Walkers particularly welcome. Book-ahead service. Special winter rates Dec - Mar. Weekly DB&B £217 - £231.

Friendly welcome, and excellent food. Recommended. AJ

Alex & Cecilia Airley
Inverour Guest House
SPEAN BRIDGE, PH34 4EU
Tel/Fax: 01397 712218
email: alex@inverour.freeserve.co.uk
web: www.fort-william.net/inverour
STB ★★★ Guest House, Walkers Welcome

41 / NN 222817 Open all year, except Christmas. Rooms: 2S, 3T, 3D. S: £20.00 pp T/D: £20.00 - £22.00 pp. Single occ. T/D: any time, £5.00 extra. Ensuite avail. with shower. No bath. B'fast 8.00am - 8.45am, early b'fast from 7.00am by arr. Packed lunches by arr. Guest lounge. Day in OK. TV in rooms & guest lounge. Drying facilities. Bike storage. Walkers particularly welcome. Book-ahead service.

Mr & Mrs L. I. Stewart
Lesanne
SPEAN BRIDGE, PH34 4EP
Tel: 01397 712231

41 / NN 219814 Open all year. Rooms: 1T, 1D, 1F. £15.00 - £20.00 pp. Single occ. T/D: off peak only, £5.00 extra. Ensuite avail. with shower. No bath. B'fast 8.30am, early b'fast from 8.00am by arr. TV in rooms. No smoking. Drying facilities.

Alan & Isabel Muir
Mahaar, Corriechoille Road
SPEAN BRIDGE, PH34 4EP
Tel: 01397 712365
email: bnb@mahaar.co.uk
web: www.mahaar.co.uk
STB ★★★ B&B

41 / NN 222815 Open all year. Rooms: 2S, 1T, 1D, 1F. S: £18.00 - £21.00 pp T/D/F: £17.00 - £20.00 pp. Single occ. T/D: any time, £5.00 - £10.00 extra. No ensuite. Bath avail. B'fast 8.00am - 9.00am, early b'fast from 7.00am by arr. Packed lunches by arr. Eve meal by arr. 6.00pm - 8.00pm, £9.00, bring your own drinks. Day in room OK. TV in rooms. Drying facilities. Bike storage. Walkers particularly welcome. Book-ahead service.

Margaret & Derek Pratt
Distant Hills Guest House
SPEAN BRIDGE, PH34 4EU
Tel/Fax: 01397 712452
email: enquiry@distanthills.com
web: www.distanthills.com
STB ★★★★ Guest House
Walkers Welcome   AA ◆◆◆◆

41 / NN 227818 Open all year, except 24th - 29th Dec. Rooms: 4T, 3D. £22.00 - £26.00 pp. Single occ. T/D: any time, £8.00 - £10.00 extra. All rooms ensuite with shower. Bath avail. B'fast 8.00am - 9.00am, early b'fast from 6.00am by arr. Packed lunches by arr. Eve meal by arr. 7.00pm - 8.00pm, £14.50, bring your own drinks. Guest lounge. Day in OK. TV in rooms & guest lounge. Drying facilities. Bike storage. Walkers particularly welcome. Book-ahead service.

Mr & Mrs S. M. Horner
Highbridge
SPEAN BRIDGE, PH34 4EX
Tel: 01397 712493
email: smh43@hotmail.com
STB ★★★ B&B, Walkers Welcome

41 / NN 199820 Open Apr - Sep. Rooms: 1T, 1D. T: £16.00 pp D: £17.00 pp. Single occ. T/D: any time, £4.00 extra. Ensuite avail. with shower/bath. Bath avail. B'fast 7.30am - 9.00am, early b'fast from 6.00am by arr. Guest lounge. Day in OK. TV in rooms & guest lounge. Drying facilities. Bike storage. Walkers particularly welcome. Book-ahead service.

Jean & Peter Wilson Tirindrish House SPEAN BRIDGE, PH34 4EU Tel: 01397 712398 Fax: 01397 712595 email: wpeterwilson@aol.com STB ★★ B&B Walkers Welcome	41 / NN 233821 Open all year, except Nov. Rooms: 1T, 1D, 1F. £17.00 -£19.00 pp.* Single occ. T/D: any time, £none - £10.00 extra. Ensuite avail. with shower & bath. Bath avail. all rooms. B'fast 8.00am - 9.00am, early b'fast from 7.00am by arr. Packed lunches by arr. Eve meal by arr. 7.00pm - 8.00pm, £12.00 (3 courses), bring your own drinks. Guest lounge. Day in OK. TV in rooms. Drying facilities. Bike storage. Book-ahead service. *Children 3 - 12 in family room: £10.00 pp.
Helen Hoare Coinachan Guest House Gairlochy Road SPEAN BRIDGE, PH34 4EG Tel: 01397 712417 Fax: 01397 712528 email: coinachan@supanet.com STB ★★★★ B&B	41 / NN 206826 Open all year, except Christmas. Rooms: 1T, 1D, 1F. £20.00 - £25.00 pp. Single occ. T/D: any time, £none - £10.00 extra. Ensuite avail. with shower. No bath. B'fast 8.00am - 8.30am, early b'fast from 7.00am by arr. Packed lunches by arr. Eve meal by arr. 7.30pm, £15.00, bring your own drinks. Guest lounge. Day in OK. TV in guest lounge. Drying facilities. Bike storage. Book-ahead service.
Justin & Lucy Swabey Corriechoille Lodge SPEAN BRIDGE, PH34 4EY Tel/Fax: 01397 712002 email: enquiry@ corriechoille.com web: www.corriechoille.com STB ★★★★ Guest House Walkers Welcome AA ◆◆◆◆	41 / NN 250806 Open Mar - Oct. Rooms: 1T, 2D, 2F. £26.00 - £27.00 pp.* Single occ. T/D: any time, £7.00 extra.** Ensuite avail. with shower/bath. Bath avail. depending on room occ. B'fast 8.00am - 9.00am, early b'fast from 7.00am by arr. Packed lunches by arr. Eve meal by arr. 7.30pm, £16.00 (3 courses). Residents licence. Guest lounge. Day in OK. TV in rooms. No smoking. Drying facilities. Bike storage. Walkers particularly welcome. *Children 7 - 13 in family room: £21.00 - £22.00 pp. **Only one room avail. for single occ. Reductions for longer stays. Self catering accommodation also avail. see www.cabins.corriechoille.com.
Gillian Cameron Mehalah Riverside House Lower Tirindrish SPEAN BRIDGE, PH34 4EU Tel/Fax: 01397 712893 Mob: 07780 928695 email: mehalahrh@gofornet.co.uk Taste of Scotland	41 / NN 228818 Open all year. Rooms: 2S, 1T, 1D. S: £18.00 - £20.00 pp T/D: £20.00 - £23.00 pp. Single occ. T/D: off peak only, £2.00 extra. Ensuite avail. with shower. Bath avail. depending on room occ. B'fast 7.45am - 8.30am, early b'fast from 7.00am by arr. Packed lunches by arr. Eve meal by arr. 7.30pm - 8.00pm, £23.00, bring your own drinks. Guest lounge. Day in OK by arr. TV in guest lounge. No smoking. Drying facilities. Bike storage. Walkers particularly welcome. Book-ahead service.

Evening/bar meals:
- Aonach Mor Hotel, SPEAN BRIDGE, PH34 4DX 01397 712351   41 / NN 219818
  Bar meals 12noon - 9.00pm; *a la carte* restaurant 6.00pm - 8.30pm. B&B from ca. £25.00 pp.
- Little Chef, SPEAN BRIDGE, PH34 4EP 01397 712297 7.00am - 10.00pm.   41 / NN 220814

Teas, etc:
- Old Station Restaurant, Station Road, SPEAN BRIDGE, PH34 4EP   41 / NN 222814
  01397 712535 Open daily except Mon, Easter - Oct, 11.00am - 5.30pm ; also open for...
  ...evening meals Fri, Sat, until 9.00pm.

Tourist info: closed at the time of publication.

Please read the entries in conjunction with the notes on pages 5 & 6.

Drumochter and Monadhliath Mountains (Sections 5 & 9)

Dalwhinnie – Laggan Bridge – Newtonmore – Kingussie
For western mountains see also Spean Bridge (Section 4)

Dalwhinnie *(Inverness-shire)*

Ann & Phil Nickson
Balsporran Cottages, Drumochter Pass
by DALWHINNIE, PH19 1AF
Tel: 01528 522389
email: ann@
    balsporran.fsbusiness.co.uk
web: www.balsporran.com

42 / NN 627792 Open all year. Rooms: 1S, 1D. £20.00 pp.
Single occ. T/D: any time, no extra. No ensuite. Bath avail.
B'fast any time by arr. Packed lunches by arr. Eve meal by arr.
from £10.00 (3 courses),* bring your own drinks. Guest lounge.
Day in OK. TV in guest lounge. Drying facilities. Bike storage.
Walkers particularly welcome. Book-ahead service. *Snacks
or only main course also avail.

The Inn at Loch Ericht
DALWHINNIE, PH19 1AG
Tel: 01528 522257
Fax: 01528 522270
email: reservations@
    priory-hotel.com
STB ★ Inn

42 / NN 637843 Open all year. Rooms: 15T, 10D, 2F. T/D: £24.50 pp
(room only: £17.50 pp) F: £49.00 - £65.00 per room (room only: £35.00 -
£55.00). Single occ. T/D: any time, no extra. All rooms ensuite with
shower/bath. Bath avail. depending on room occ. B'fast 7.30am - 11.00am,
early b'fast from 6.30am by arr. Packed lunches by arr. Meals 7.30am -
9.00pm. Full licence. Guest lounge. Day in OK. TV in rooms. Drying
facilities. Bike storage. Walkers particularly welcome. Book-ahead service.

Evening/bar meals:
– The Inn at Loch Ericht *(see main entry)*

Laggan Bridge *(Inverness-shire)*

Monadhliath Hotel, Laggan Bridge
NEWTONMORE, PH20 1BT
Tel/Fax: 01528 544276
email: monadhliath@
    lagganbridge.com
web: www.lagganbridge.com
STB ★★★ Small Hotel
Walkers Welcome

35 / NN 616938 Open all year. Rooms: 4T, 4D. £25.00 - £28.00 pp.
Single occ. T/D: any time, £5.00 extra. Ensuite avail. with shower.
No bath. B'fast 8.00am - 9.00am, early b'fast from 7.30am by arr.*
Packed lunches by arr. Eve meals 6.00pm - 9.00pm. Full licence.
Guest lounge. Day in OK. TV in rooms & guest lounge. Drying
facilities. Bike storage. Walkers particularly welcome. Book-ahead
service. Rates avail. for DB&B. Reductions for special winter/spring
breaks. *Continental b'fast avail. earlier by arr.

Newtonmore *(Inverness-shire)*

Christine & Duncan Watson
Glenquoich House, Glen Road
NEWTONMORE, PH20 1DZ
Tel/Fax: 01540 673461
email: efb007@aol.com
STB ★★★ Guest House
Walkers Welcome

35 / NN 714993 Open all year. Rooms: 1S, 2T, 1D, 1F.
S: £18.00 pp T/D/F: £18.50 pp. Single occ. T/D: any time, £5.00
extra. Ensuite avail. with shower. No bath. B'fast 8.00am -
9.00am, early b'fast from 7.30am by arr. Packed lunches by arr.
Guest lounge. Day in OK. TV in rooms & guest lounge. No
smoking. Drying facilities. Bike storage. Walkers particularly
welcome. Book-ahead service.

Nicky & Geoff Drucquer
Eagle View Guest House, Perth Road
NEWTONMORE, PH20 1AP
Tel/Fax: 01540 673675
email: eagview@aol.com
web: www.newtonmore.com/eagleview
STB ★★★ Guest House
Taste of Scotland

35 / NN 712988   Open all year. Rooms: 1S, 1T, 2D, 1F. £20.00 pp.* Single occ. T/D: off peak only, £none - £10.00 extra. Ensuite avail. with shower. No bath. B'fast 8.00am - 9.30am, early b'fast from 7.30am by arr. Packed lunches by arr. Eve meal by arr. £17.50, bring your own drinks. Guest lounge. TV in rooms. No smoking. Drying facilities. Bike storage. Walkers particularly welcome. Book-ahead service. *Children under 12 in family room: half price.

Friendly welcome, and the best scrambled eggs I have ever had. Recommended. AJ

Pam & Colin Walker
The Pines, Station Road
NEWTONMORE
PH20 1AR
Tel: 01540 673271
Fax: 01540 673882
web: www.smoothhound
      .co.uk /hotels/thepines

35 / NN 713985   Open all year, except Christmas. Rooms: 2S, 2T, 2D. £19.00 - £24.00 pp Single occ. T/D: any time,* no extra. Ensuite avail. with shower/bath. Bath avail. depending on room occ. B'fast 8.00am - 8.45am, early b'fast from 6.45am by arr. Packed lunches by arr. Eve meal by arr. 7.00pm, £14.75. Residents licence (meals only). Guest lounge. Day in OK. TV in rooms. No smoking. Drying facilities. Bike storage. Walkers particularly welcome. Book-ahead service. *Restricted at N.Year & first week in August. Hosts will meet guests arriving by public transport.

Evening/bar meals:
– Glen Hotel, Main Street, NEWTONMORE, PH20 1DD 01540 673203   35 / NN 713989
   Bar meals all day until 9.00pm, home-made pizzas to 11.00pm. B&B from around £20.00 pp.
– Braeriach Hotel, Main Street, NEWTONMORE, PH20 1DA 01540 673279   35 / NN 714990
   Bar meals 11.00am - 9.00pm. B&B from around £20.00 pp.
– Capercaillie Restaurant, Main Street, NEWTONMORE, PH20 1DA   35 / NN 715991
   01540 673231 capercaillie@Flight.prestel.co.uk www.capercaillierestaurant.com
   Open daily except Mon, Mar - Dec, 11.30am - 2.30pm, 6.00pm - 9.00pm.
Teas etc:
– Toshac's Tuck Shop & Tea Room, Main Street, NEWTONMORE   35 / NN 715991
   015540 673427 Open daily, 10.00am - 6.00pm, open later in summer.

Kingussie *(Inverness-shire)*

Anne & Mark Johnstone
Greystones B&B, Acres Road
KINGUSSIE, PH21 1LA
Tel: 01540 661052
Fax: 01540 662162
email: Greystones@surf.to
web: www.surf.to/greystones

35 / NH 758011   Open all year. Rooms: 1S, 1T, 1D, 1F. £25.00 pp. Single occ. T/D: any time, no extra. No ensuite. Bath avail. B'fast 7.00am - 10.00am, early b'fast by arr. Packed lunches by arr. Bring your own eve meal & drinks. Guest lounge. Day in OK. TV in rooms & guest lounge. No smoking. Drying facilities. Bike storage. Walkers particularly welcome. Book- ahead service.

Janet & Roger Crawford
Glengarry, East Terrace
KINGUSSIE, PH21 1JS
Tel/Fax: 01540 661386
email: glengarry@scot89.freeserve.co.uk
web: www.scot89.freeserve.co.uk
STB ★★★★ B&B, Walkers Welcome

35 / NH 759009   Open all year. Rooms: 1S, 1T, 2D. £23.00 pp. Single occ. T/D: any time, £7.00 extra. Ensuite avail. with shower/bath. Bath avail. depending on room occ. B'fast 8.30am, early b'fast from 7.00am by arr. Packed lunches by arr. Eve meal by arr. 7.00pm, £15.00, bring your own drinks. Guest lounge. Day in OK. TV in rooms. No smoking. Drying facilities. Bike storage. Book-ahead service.

Drumochter, Monadhliath, South Grampian & Cairngorm Mountains (Sections 5 & 9, Sections 6 & 7, Section 8)

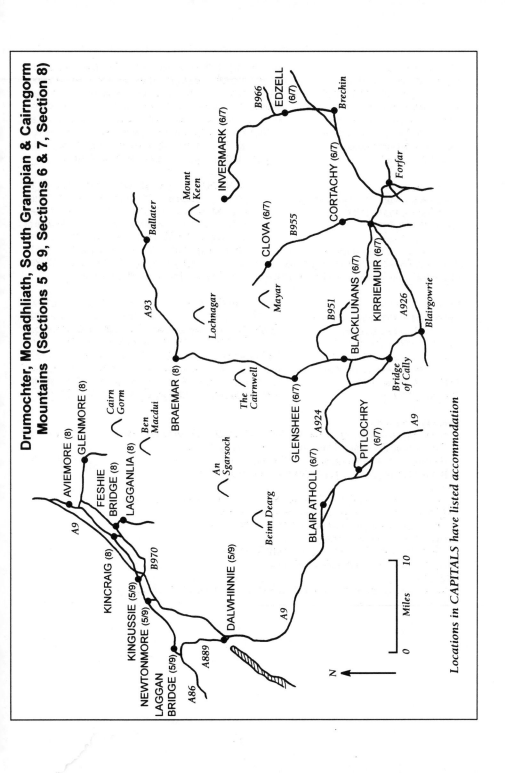

Locations in CAPITALS have listed accommodation

David & Marie Taylor
The Hermitage Guest House
Spey Street, KINGUSSIE, PH21 1HN
Tel: 01540 662137 Fax: 01540 662177
email: thehermitage@clara.net
web: www.thehermitage-scotland.com
STB ★★★★ Guest House
Walkers Welcome

35 / NH 758005 Open all year, except 1st - 15th Nov. Rooms: 2T, 3D. £22.00 - £24.00 pp. Single occ. T/D: any time, £5.00 - £10.00 extra. Ensuite avail. with shower/bath. Bath avail. depending on room occ. B'fast 8.00am - 9.00am, early b'fast from 7.00am by arr. Packed lunches by arr. Eve meal by arr. 7.00pm, £13.00 (3 courses). Residents licence. Guest lounge. Day in OK. TV in rooms. No smoking. Drying facilities. Bike storage. Walkers particularly welcome. Book-ahead service.

Jennifer Anderson
Homewood Lodge, Newtonmore Road
KINGUSSIE, PH21 1HD
Tel: 01540 661507
email: enquiries@
    homewood-lodge-kingussie.co.uk
web: www.homewood-lodge-kingussie.co.uk
STB ★★★★ Guest House, Walkers Welcome

35 / NH 752005 Open all year. Rooms: 1T, 2D, 1F. £20.00 pp. Single occ. T/D: any time, no extra. Ensuite avail. with shower. No bath. B'fast 7.30am - 8.30am, early b'fast by arr. Packed lunches by arr. Eve meal by arr. 6.00pm, £10.00, bring your own drinks. Guest lounge. Day in OK. TV in rooms & guest lounge. No smoking. Drying facilities. Bike storage. Walkers particularly welcome. Book-ahead service.

David & Tricia Spry
Arden House, Newtonmore Road
KINGUSSIE, PH21 1HE
Tel/Fax: 01540 661369
email: ardenhouse@compuserve.com
web: www.kingussie.co.uk/ardenhouse
STB ★★★ Guest House
Walkers Welcome

35 / NH 755006 Open all year. Rooms: 1T, 3D, 1F. £18.00 - £22.50 pp. Single occ. T/D: any time, £none - £3.00 extra.* Ensuite avail. with shower/bath. Bath avail. depending on room occ. B'fast 8.30am - 9.00am, early b'fast from 7.00am by arr. Packed lunches by arr. Eve meal by arr. 7.00pm, £10.00, bring your own drinks. Guest lounge. Day in OK. TV in rooms & guest lounge. No smoking. Drying facilities. Bike storage. Book-ahead service. *Charged Easter - Oct, Xmas & N.Year.

Evening/bar meals:
- The Royal Hotel, 29 High Street, KINGUSSIE, PH21 1HX 01540 661898   35 / NH 758007
  Bar meals all day until 9.30pm. B&B from around £25.00 pp.
- Star Hotel, 32 High Street, KINGUSSIE, PH21 1HR 01540 661431   35 / NH 758006
  Bar meals 6.00pm - 8.45pm. B&B from around £23.00 pp.

Teas etc:
- Gilly's Kitchen, 57 High St, KINGUSSIE 01540 662273 Open Mon - Sat,
  10.00am - 5.00pm. Light lunches served until 4.00pm.
- Pam's Café, 54 High Street, KINGUSSIE 01540 661020
  Open daily 10.00am - 5.00pm.
- Volante's Café, 19 High St, KINGUSSIE 01540 661346
  Open daily except Tue, 12noon - 9.00pm.

Bike hire:
- Service Sports, 26 High Street, KINGUSSIE, PH21 1HR 01540 661228

South Grampian Mountains (Sections 6 & 7)

Blair Atholl – Pitlochry – Blacklunans – Glenshee – Kirriemuir – Cortachy – Clova
Edzell – Invermark

Blair Atholl *(Perthshire)*

Mrs Sandy Pywell Dalgreine Guest House, Blair Atholl PITLOCHRY, PH18 5SX Tel/Fax: 01796 481276 email: mail@ dalgreine-guest-house.co.uk web: www.dalgreine-guest-house.co.uk STB ★★★ Guest House Walkers Welcome AA ◆◆◆◆	43 / NN 878653 Open all year. Rooms: 1S, 2T, 2D, 1F. S: £18.00 pp T/D: £18.00 - £22.00 pp F: £55.00 - £66.00 per room. Single occ. T/D: any time, £7.00 extra. Ensuite avail. with shower. Bath avail. B'fast 8.00am - 8.30am, early b'fast any time by arr. Packed lunches by arr. Eve meal by arr. 6.30pm - 7.30pm, £10.00 (2 courses) - £12.00 (3 courses), bring your own drinks. Guest lounge. Day in OK. TV in guest lounge. No smoking. Drying facilities. Bike storage. Walkers particularly welcome. Book-ahead service.
Kirstie & Geoff Crerar The Firs, St Andrews Crescent Blair Atholl PITLOCHRY, PH18 5TA Tel: 01796 481256 Fax: 01796 481661 email: kirstie@firs-blairatholl.co.uk web: www.firs-blairatholl.co.uk STB ★★★ Guest House	43 / NN 877652 Open all year. Rooms: 3T, 2D, 2F. T/D: £20.00 - £25.00 pp F: £20.00 - £25.00 per adult. Single occ. T/D: any time, £5.00 extra. Ensuite avail. with shower/bath. Bath avail. depending on room occ. B'fast 8.15am - 9.00am, early b'fast from 7.30am by arr. Packed lunches by arr. Eve meal by arr. Nov - Mar 7.30pm, £12.50, bring your own drinks. Guest lounge. Day in OK. TV in rooms. Drying facilities. Bike storage. Book-ahead service. Off-peak offer 2 sharing for 2 nights £75.00 incl. packed lunch.
Mrs Steindl Beechwood, The Terrace Blair Atholl PITLOCHRY, PH18 5SZ Tel: 01796 481379 STB ★★ B&B	43 / NN 878651 Open all year, except Christmas. Rooms: 1T, 2D. £19.00 pp. No single occ. T/D. Ensuite avail. with shower/bath. Bath avail. depending on room occ. B'fast 7.30am - 9.30am, early b'fast from 7.00am by arr. Packed lunches by arr. Eve meal by arr. 5.30pm - 7.00pm, £10.00. Day in room OK. TV in rooms. No smoking. Drying facilities. Bike storage. Walkers particularly welcome. Book-ahead service.
Gordon & Lin Muirhead Ptarmigan House, Blair Atholl PITLOCHRY, PH18 5SZ Tel/Fax: 01796 481269 email: gordon@ptarmiganhouse.co.uk web: www.ptarmiganhouse.co.uk STB ★★★ Guest House	43 / NN 878651 Open all year. Rooms: 2T, 4D, 2F. T: £22.00 - £30.00 pp D: £20.00 - £25.00 pp F: £52.00 - £64.00 per room. Single occ. T/D: off peak only, £10.00 extra. Ensuite avail. with shower. No bath. B'fast 8.00am - 9.00am, early b'fast from 6.00am by arr. Packed lunches by arr. Residents licence. Day in room OK. TV in rooms. No smoking. Drying facilities. Bike storage. Book-ahead service.

Evening/bar meals:
- Bothy Bar, Atholl Arms Hotel, Blair Atholl, PITLOCHRY, PH18 5SG   43 / NN 871653
  01796 481205 Bar meals all day until 9.30pm. B&B from around £30.00 pp.
- Bridge of Tilt Hotel, Blair Atholl, PITLOCHRY, PH18 5SU 01796 481333   43 / NN 877654
  Bar meals 6.00pm - 8.30pm. B&B from around £33.00 pp.

Teas etc:
- Blair Atholl Water Mill & Tea Room, Ford Road, Blair Atholl, PITLOCHRY   43 / NN 872652
  PH18 5SH 01796 481321 Open daily, Easter - Oct: 10.00am - 5.30pm (Mon - Sat),
  12.00noon - 5.30pm (Sun). Homebaking using own flour & oatmeal, light snacks.

Bike hire:
- Atholl Mountain Bike Hire, Old School Park, Blair Atholl, PITLOCHRY, PH18 5SP
01796 481646 (Daytime, Easter - mid Oct) 01796 473553 (All year)

Pitlochry *(Perthshire)*

Helen Fox & Brian Stone
Carra Beag Guest House
16 Toberargan Road
PITLOCHRY, PH16 5HG
Tel/Fax: 01796 472835
email: visitus@carrabeag.co.uk
web: www.carrabeag.co.uk
STB ★★★ Guest House
Walkers Welcome

52 / NN 942582 Open Feb - Nov. Rooms: 4S, 3T, 3D, 2F. £16.00 - £24.00 pp. Single occ. T/D: any time, £none - £15.00 extra. Ensuite avail. with shower/bath. Bath avail. B'fast 8.15am - 9.30am, early b'fast from 5.00am by arr. Packed lunches by arr. Eve meal by arr. for groups of 10 or more, 6.30pm - 7.30pm, £13.50 (3 courses). Residents licence. Guest lounge. Day in OK. TV in rooms. No smoking. Drying facilities. Bike storage. Walkers particularly welcome. Book-ahead service.

Barbara & David Braine
Dundarave House, Strathview Terrace
PITLOCHRY, PH16 5AT
Tel/Fax: 01796 473109
email: dundarave.guesthouse@
        virgin.net
web: www.smoothhound.co.uk
        /hotels/dundarave.html
STB ★★★ Guest House   AA ◆◆◆◆

52 / NN 938584 Open all year, except Christmas/ N.Year. Rooms: 2S, 3T, 5D, 2F. S: £18.00 - £22.00 pp T/D: £20.00 - £25.00 pp F: £50.00 - £75.00 per room. Single occ. T/D: off peak only, £5.00 extra. Ensuite avail. with shower/bath. Bath avail. depending on room occ. B'fast 8.15am - 9.00am, early b'fast from 8.00am by arr. Packed lunches by arr. Eve meal by arr. 6.30pm, £12.00, bring your own drinks. Guest lounge. Day in OK. TV in rooms. No smoking. Drying facilities. Bike storage.

Derek & Marion Stephenson
Derrybeg Guest House
18 Lower Oakfield
PITLOCHRY, PH16 5DS
Tel/Fax: 01796 472070
STB ★★★★ Guest House

52 / NN 943581 Open Jan - Nov. Rooms: 2S, 6T, 9D* £20.00 - £27.00 pp Single occ. T/D: any time, up to £16.50 extra. All rooms ensuite with shower/bath. Bath avail. depending on room occ. B'fast 8.15am - 9.00am. Eve meal by arr. 6.15pm - 6.45pm, £15.00 (4 courses), bring your own drinks. Guest lounge. Day in OK. TV in rooms. Drying facilities. Bike storage. Book-ahead service. *Bed arrangement adaptable.

And many more places to stay in Pitlochry.

Evening/bar meals: plenty of choice in Pitlochry.
Bike hire:
- Escape Route, 8 West Moulin Road, PITLOCHRY, PH16 5AD 01796 473859
Tourist info: 22 Atholl Road, PITLOCHRY, PH16 5DB 01796 472215/472751 (All year)

Blacklunans *(Perthshire)*

Mrs Morag Houston
Glenkilrie
Blacklunans
by BLAIRGOWRIE
PH10 7LR
Tel: 01250 882241

43 / NO 137605   Open all year, except Christmas.   Rooms: 1T, 2D. £15.00/£17.00 pp. Single occ. T/D: any time, £2.00 extra. Ensuite avail. with bath. Bath avail. depending on room occ. B'fast 8.00am - 9.30am, early b'fast any time by arr. Packed lunches by arr. Eve meal by arr. 6.00pm - 8.00pm, £7.50, bring your own drinks. Guest lounge. Day in OK. TV in guest lounge. No smoking. Drying facilities. Bike storage. Book-ahead service.

Evening/bar meals:
- Dalrulzion Hotel & Coffee Stop, Blackwater, Bridge of Cally, BLAIRGOWRIE 53 / NO 137589 PH10 7LJ 01250 882222 Bar meals 6.00pm - 8.00pm. B&B from around £25.00 pp.

Teas etc:
- Coffee Stop at the Dalrulzion Hotel *(see above)* Open daily, 11.00am - 5.00pm.

Bike hire:
- Crighton's Cycles, 87 Perth St, BLAIRGOWRIE, PH10 6DT 01250 874447

Glenshee *(Perthshire)*

Cairnwell Mountain Sports	43 / NO 109702 Open all year. Rooms: 2T, 1D, 2F.
Gulabin Lodge, Glenshee	T/D: £14.00 - £15.00 pp F: £40.00 per room. Single occ.
by BLAIRGOWRIE, PH10 7QE	T/D: any time, £5.00 extra. No ensuite. No bath,
Tel/Fax: 0870 443 0253 (office)	showers only. B'fast 7.45am - 8.30am, early b'fast by
Tel: 0870 443 0254 (lodge)	arr. Eve meal by arr, £6.00 - £8.00, bring your own
Mob: 07778 941687	drinks. Guest lounge. Day in OK. No TV. No smoking.
email: info@cairnwellmountainsports.co.uk	Drying facilities. Bike storage. Walkers particularly
web: www.cairnwellmountainsports.co.uk	welcome. Book-ahead service. Group rooms also avail.
/gulabin_lodge.htm	Self catering £12.00 pp.

Evening/bar meals:
- Spittal of Glenshee Hotel, Glenshee, by BLAIRGOWRIE, PH10 7QF   43 / NO 110699 01250 885215 www.spittalofglenshee.co.uk Bar meals until 5.30pm, buffet meals...
...6.30pm - 8.15pm. B&B from around £29.00 pp.

Kirriemuir *(Angus)*

Mrs Jessma Lindsay	54 / NO 380544 Open all year. Rooms: 1S, 1T, 1D. £23.00 pp.
Crepto, 1 Kinnordy Place	Single occ. T/D: any time, £5.00 extra. No ensuite. Bath avail.
KIRRIEMUIR, DD8 4JW	B'fast 7.00am - 9.00am, early b'fast by arr. Packed lunches by
Tel: 01575 572746	arr. Guest lounge. TV in rooms & guest lounge. No smoking.
email: davendjessma@bun.com	Drying facilities. Bike storage. Book-ahead service.
STB ★★ B&B	

Mrs Flora Sillence	54 / NO 393542 Open all year, except Christmas. Rooms:
Woodlands, 2 Lisden Gardens	1S, 1T, 1D. £22.00 pp. No single occ. T/D. No ensuite.
Brechin Road, KIRRIEMUIR, DD8 4DW	Bath avail. depending on room occ. B'fast 7.00am -
Tel/Fax: 01575 572582	9.00am, early b'fast from 6.00am by arr. Packed lunches by
Mob: 07710 206571	arr. Eve meal by arr. £12.00, bring your own drinks. Guest
email: woodlands@faxvia.net	lounge. TV in rooms & guest lounge. No smoking. Drying
STB ★★★★ B&B	facilities. Bike storage. Book-ahead service.

Evening/bar meals:
- Airlie Arms Hotel, St Malcolms Wynd, KIRRIEMUIR, DD8 4HB   54 / NO 385540 01575 572847 info@airliearms-hotel.co.uk www.airliearms-hotel.co.uk Bar meals 5.00pm - 8.00pm. B&B from around £25.00 pp.

Cortachy *(Angus)*

Susan Mclaren
Muirhouses Farm, Cortachy
KIRRIEMUIR, DD8 4QG
Tel: 01575 573128
email: muirhousesfarm@farming.me.uk
STB ★★★ B&B

54 / NO 392566 Open all year, except Christmas, Jan, Feb. Rooms: 1T, 1D, 1F. £20.00 pp. Single occ. T/D: off peak only, £5.00 extra. No ensuite. Bath avail. B'fast 7.00am - 9.00am, early b'fast from 6.00am by arr. Packed lunches by arr. TV in rooms. No smoking. Drying facilities. Bike storage. Walkers particularly welcome. Book-ahead service.

Evening/bar meals: see Kirriemuir

Clova *(Angus)*

Glen Clova Hotel
Glen Clova
by KIRRIEMUIR
DD8 4QS
Tel: 01575 550350
email: hotel@clova.com
web: www.clova.com
STB ★★★ Small Hotel

44 / NO 327731 Open all year, except 25th Dec. Rooms: 5T, 5D. T: £35.00 - £39.50 pp D: £30.00 - £35.00 pp. Single occ. T/D: any time, £5.00 extra. Ensuite avail. with shower/bath. Bath avail. B'fast 8.00am - 9.30am, early b'fast from 7.30am by arr. Packed lunches by arr. Meals 12.00 noon - 9.00pm. Full licence. Guest lounge. Day in OK. TV in rooms. Drying facilities. Bike storage. Walkers particularly welcome. Book-ahead service. Mid-week special offers Oct - Apr. Bunkhouse avail. £9.50 pp incl. bedding, communal kitchen.

Edzell *(Angus)*

J. & E. Cameron
Doune House, 24 High Street
Edzell, BRECHIN, DD9 7TA
Tel: 01356 648201
email: johna@
     cameron21.freeserve.co.uk
web: www.dounehouse.edzell.org.uk
STB ★★★ B&B

45 / NO 601689   Open all year, except Christmas/N.Year. Rooms: 1T, 1D, 1F. T: £17.00 pp D: £16.00 pp F: £50.00 per room.* Single occ. T/D: any time, £1.00 - £2.00 extra. No ensuite.** Bath avail. depending on room occ. B'fast 8.00am - 9.00am, early b'fast from 7.00am by arr. Packed lunches by arr. Day in room OK. TV in rooms. No smoking. Drying facilities. Book-ahead service. *F room rate depends on age, room also avail. as T (£19.00 pp) or D (£18.00 pp) **Private facilities avail.

Mrs A. McMurray
Inchcape Bed & Breakfast
High Street
Edzell, BRECHIN, DD9 7TF
Tel: 01356 647266
email: alison.mcm@btinternet.com
STB ★★★ B&B

45 / NO 602686 Open all year. Rooms: 1S, 1T, 1F. S: £20.00 pp T/F: £18.00 pp.* Single occ. T/D: any time, no extra. Ensuite avail. with shower. No bath. B'fast 8.00am - 8.30am, early b'fast from 7.00am by arr. Packed lunches by arr. Guest lounge. Day in OK. TV in guest lounge. No smoking. Drying facilities. Bike storage. Walkers particularly welcome. Book-ahead service. *Children in family room: £9.00 pp.

34

Adam & Frances McGill	45 / NO 601689 Open all year. Rooms: 1S, 1T, 1D. £18.00 -
North Esk Lodge	£20.00 pp. Single occ. T/D: any time, £none - £5.00 extra. Ensuite
18A High Street	avail. with shower. Bath avail. all rooms. B'fast 8.00am - 9.30am,
Edzell, BRECHIN, DD9 7TA	early b'fast by arr. Packed lunches by arr. Guest lounge. Day in OK.
Tel: 01356 647409	TV in guest lounge. Drying facilities. Bike storage. Book-ahead
STB ★★★ B&B	service.

Evening/bar meals:
- Panmure Arms Hotel, 52 High Street, Edzell, BRECHIN, DD9 7TA   45 / NO 600691
  01356 648950 david@panmurearmshotel.co.uk www.panmurearmshotel.co.uk
  Bar meals 5.30pm - 8.45pm (Mon - Fri), 12noon - 9.00pm (Sat, Sun). B&B from ca. £30.00 pp.
- Glenesk Hotel & Country Club, High Street, Edzell, BRECHIN, DD9 7TF   45 / NO 601685
  01356 648319 Bar meals 7.30pm - 9.15pm. B&B from around £49.00 pp.
- Tuck Inn, 44 High Street, Edzell, BRECHIN, DD9 7TA 01356 648262   45 / NO 600690
  Open daily, 11.00am - 8.00pm (Sun - Fri), 11.00am - 9.00pm (Sat). Closing times quoted are for
  take-away, last orders to eat in 30mins earlier.

Teas etc:
- Picturesque Art Gallery & Coffee Shop, 40A High Street, Edzell, BRECHIN   45 / NO 600690
  DD9 7TA 01356 648699 Open daily, 9.00am - 5.00pm (Mon - Sat), 12noon - 5.00pm (Sun).

Invermark (Angus)

Ms Bea Rawlinson	44 / NO 444806 Open all year. Rooms: 2T, 1D. T: £26.00 -
The House of Mark Guest House	£28.00 pp D: £30.00 pp. Single occ. T/D: any time, no extra.
Invermark	Ensuite avail. with shower. Bath (2) avail. all rooms. B'fast 7.00am -
Glenesk, by BRECHIN	9.00am, early b'fast by arr. Packed lunches by arr. Eve meal by
DD9 7YZ	arr. 6.00pm - 9.00pm, £17.00, bring your own drinks. Guest lounge.
Tel: 01356 670315	Day in OK. TV in guest lounge. No smoking. Drying facilities. Bike
web: www.thehouseofmark.com	storage. Book-ahead service. Reductions for longer stays.

Evening/bar meals: see also Edzell, but it's a long way away...

Brain-teaser.

How many names of Munros can you make from the letters of THE MUNRO-
BAGGER'S BED AND BREAKFAST GUIDE ?   (Not forgetting the hyphen and
apostrophe.)

Well, for a start there's Sgor Gaibhre. No prizes for any others, just the fun of it.

Cairngorm Mountains (Section 8)

Braemar – Kincraig – Feshie Bridge – Lagganlia – Aviemore – Glenmore

Braemar *(Aberdeenshire)*

Dennis & Fairlie Sharp Balnellan House, Glenshee Road Braemar, BALLATER AB35 5YQ Tel: 013397 41474 email: balnellan@hotmail.com web: www.geocities.com /thetropics/4921	43 / NO 152912 Open all year, except Christmas/N.Year. Rooms: 1T, 2D. £24.00 pp. Single occ. T/D: any time, £6.00 extra. Ensuite avail. with shower/bath. Bath avail. depending on room occ. B'fast 8.00am, early b'fast from 7.00am by arr. Packed lunches by arr. Eve meal by arr. 7.30pm - 8.30pm, £15.00, bring your own drinks. Guest lounge. Day in OK by arr. TV in guest lounge. No smoking. Drying facilities. Bike storage. Walkers particularly welcome. Book-ahead service.

Mrs Sue Elliott Comely Bank, 20 Cairnadrochit Braemar, BALLATER AB35 5YS Tel: 013397 41553 email: comelybank@ talk21.com STB ★★ B&B	43 / NO 150915 Open all year. Rooms: 1S, 1T*,1D. £15.00 - £18.00 pp. Single occ. T/D: off peak only, £6.00 extra. No ensuite. Bath avail. B'fast 8.00am - 8.45pm, early b'fast from 7.30am by arr. Packed lunches by arr. Eve meal by arr. 6.00pm - 6.30pm, £7.50, bring your own drinks. Guest lounge. Day in OK. TV in rooms. No smoking. Drying facilities. Bike storage. Walkers particularly welcome. Book-ahead service. Reduction for weekly rates. Children and pets welcome. *Converts to family room, children 3 - 12 half price.

Friendly welcome and a good breakfast. Don't miss the mushrooms on the back lawn. Recommended. AJ

Mrs Ingerlise C. McKellar Morningside Kindrochit Drive Braemar, BALLATER AB35 5YW Tel: 013397 41370	43 / NO 153913 Open all year. Rooms: 1T, 1D. £17.00 pp. Single occ. T/D: any time, £3.00 extra. No ensuite. Bath avail. B'fast 7.30am - 9.30am, early b'fast by arr. Packed lunches by arr. Eve meal by arr. 6.30pm - 9.00pm, £8.00 - £10.00, bring your own drinks. Guest lounge. Day in OK. TV in guest lounge. Drying facilities. Bike storage. Well-behaved dogs welcome.

Moorfield House Hotel Chapel Brae Braemar, BALLATER AB35 5YT Tel: 013397 41244	43 / NO 146912 Open all year. Rooms: 1S, 1T, 1D, 2F. £17.00 pp. Single occ. T/D: any time, no extra. Ensuite avail. with shower. Bath avail. B'fast 8.15am - 8.45am, early b'fast from 7.30am by arr. Packed lunches by arr. Eve meals 6.00pm - 9.00pm (dinner or bar meals). Full licence. Day in OK. TV in lounge bar. Drying facilities. Bike storage. Book-ahead service (not local). Rates negotiable for groups or longer stays. Resident proprietors.

Friendly welcome and good food. Recommended. AJ

Julie & Steven Heyes Schiehallion House Glenshee Road Braemar, BALLATER · AB35 5YQ Tel: 013397 41679 STB ★★★ Guest House	43 / NO 153911 Open Jan - Sep. Rooms: 1S, 3T, 3D, 2F. S: £20.00 pp T/D: £18.00 - £21.00 pp F: £18.00 - £19.00 per adult.* Single occ. T/D: off peak only, £5.00 - £10.00 extra. Ensuite avail. with shower. Bath avail. depending on room occ. B'fast 7.45am - 8.30am, early b'fast from 7.30am by arr. Packed lunches by arr. Guest lounge. Day in OK. TV in guest lounge. Drying facilities. Bike storage. Walkers particularly welcome. Book-ahead service. Hillwalking proprietors. *Children up to 14 in family room: £1.00 per year of age (minimum £6.00).

Anne Robson Dalmore House, Fife Brae Braemar, BALLATER AB35 5NS Tel: 013397 41225 email: dalmorehouse@ yahoo.com web: www.dalmorehouse.co.uk STB ★★★ B&B	43 / NO 150914 Open all year. Rooms: 2T, 1D. £17.00 - £22.00 pp. Single occ. T/D: any time, £none - £8.00 extra.* Ensuite avail. with shower. Bath avail. B'fast 7.00am - 9.00am, early b'fast from 6.00am by arr. Packed lunches by arr. Guest lounge. Day in OK. TV in guest lounge & double room. Drying facilities. Walkers particularly welcome. Book-ahead service. Munroist proprietor. Package breaks incl. DB&B, packed lunch, transport. One mountain bike avail. to guests. Self-catering annex (STB ★★★) sleeps 3, with lounge area, price includes towels, linen, electricity. *Normally no single supplement charged.

Evening/bar meals:
- Moorfield House Hotel *(see main entry)*
- Fife Arms Hotel, Mar Road, Braemar, BALLATER, AB35 5YL 013397 41644 43 / NO 150914
  Bar meals 6.00pm - 8.30pm; *a la carte* restaurant 7.00pm - 8.00pm. B&B from ca. £25.00 pp.
- Braemar Lodge Hotel, Glenshee Road, Braemar, BALLATER, AB35 5YQ   43 / NO 152912
  013397 41627 www.braemarlodge.co.uk *A la carte* restaurant 6.00pm - 8.45pm.
  B&B from around £25.00 pp
- The Gathering Place, Invercauld Road, Braemar, BALLATER, AB35 5YP   43 / NO 151914
  013397 41234 www.the-gathering-place.co.uk Open 10.00am - 11:00pm but food last orders
  at 9.00pm. (Open Wed - Sat at time of publication, expects to go to 7 day opening.)
- Invercauld Arms Hotel *(no longer does bar meals and has closed its public bar since being taken over as a coach tours hotel by Shearings)*

Teas etc:
- Gordons Tearoom & Restaurant, 20 Mar Road, Braemar, BALLATER,   43 / NO150914
  AB35 5YL 013397 41247 Open daily, 10.30am - 4.30pm (Dec - Apr); 10.30am - 6.00pm
  (May - mid Jun, mid Sep - Oct); 10.00am - 8.00pm (mid Jun - mid Sep), closed Nov.
- The Old Bakery Coffee Shop & Restaurant, 18 Mar Road, Braemar   43 / NO150914
  BALLATER, AB35 5YL 013397 41415 Open daily except Fri, 9.30am - 5.30pm...
  (Easter - Autumn); open Sat, Sun, Mon, Tues, 10.00am - 3.00pm (Winter).

Bike hire:
- Braemar Mountain Sports, Invercauld Road, Braemar, BALLATER, AB35 5YP
  013397 41242 www.freeheeldirect.com Open 8.30am - 6.00pm (Mon - Thu),
  8.30am - 7.00pm (Fri - Sun)

Tourist info: The Mews, Mar Road, Braemar, BALLATER, AB35 5YL 013397 41600 (All year)

Kincraig *(Inverness-shire)*

The Ossian Hotel The Brae, Kincraig by KINGUSSIE, PH21 1QD Tel: 01540 651242 Fax: 01540 651633 Mob: 07773 103595 email: ossian@kincraig.com web: www.kincraig.com /ossian.htm	35 / NH 831057 Open all year, except Nov & Jan. Rooms: 2S, 2T, 3D, 2F. £25.00 - £30.00 pp.* Single occ. T/D: any time, no extra. All rooms ensuite with shower & bath except 1F (private shower/bath) 1S (shower). B'fast 8.00am - 9.00am, early b'fast from 7.30am by arr.** Packed lunches by arr. Eve meals: *a la carte* dinner 7.30pm - 9.30pm, from £17.00 (4 courses). Full licence. Guest lounge. Day in OK. TV in rooms. Drying facilities. Bike storage. Walkers particularly welcome. Book-ahead service. *Reduced room rate if dinner taken at hotel. **Continental b'fast avail. earlier by arr. Reductions for longer stays

Please read the entries in conjunction with the notes on pages 5 & 6.

Nick & Patsy Thompson
Insh House Guest House
Kincraig, by KINGUSSIE
PH21 1NU
Tel: 01540 651377
email: Inshhouse@btinternet.com
web: www.kincraig.com
/inshhouse.htm
STB ★★★ Guest House

35 / NH 836038 Open Jan - Oct. Rooms: 2S, 1T, 1D, 1F. S: £18.00 - £19.00 pp T: £18.00 - £21.00 pp D: £20.00 - £22.00 pp F: £50.00 - £60.00 per room. Single occ. T/D: off peak only, no extra. Ensuite avail. with shower. Bath avail. B'fast 8.00am - 9.00am, early b'fast from 7.00am by arr. Packed lunches by arr. Eve meal by arr. 7.00pm, £10.00 - £11.00, bring your own drinks. Guest lounge. Day in OK. TV in guest lounge. No smoking. Drying facilities. Bike storage. Walkers particularly welcome. Book-ahead service. House named on OS Landranger sheet 35.

Guy & Fiona Johnson
Braeriach Guest House
Braeriach Road
Kincraig, by KINGUSSIE
PH21 1QA
Tel: 01540 651369
STB ★★★ Guest House

35 / NH 834057 Open all year. Rooms: 2T, 3D. £24.00 - £28.00 pp. Single occ. T/D: any time, no extra. All rooms ensuite with shower/bath. Bath avail. B'fast 8.00am - 9.30am, early b'fast from 7.00am by arr. Packed lunches by arr. Eve meal by arr. 7.00pm - 8.30pm, £18.00, bring your own drinks. Guest lounge. Day in OK. TV in guest lounge. No smoking. Drying facilities. Bike storage. Walkers particularly welcome. Book-ahead service.

The Suie Hotel
Kincraig, by KINGUSSIE
PH21 1NA
Tel: 01540 651344
Fax: 01540 651586
email: suiehotel@barbox.net
web: www.kincraig.com/suie
STB ★★★ Guest House

35 / NH 830057 Open all year. Rooms: 1S, 2T, 2D, 3F. S: £29.50 pp T/D: from £22.50 pp F: £60.00 per room (based on 4 sharing). Single occ. T/D: off peak only, no extra. Ensuite avail. with shower/bath. Bath avail. B'fast 8.00am - 9.00am, early b'fast from 6.30am by arr. Packed lunches by arr. Eve meal by arr. 7.00pm - 9.00pm, from £4.95 (bar supper). Full licence. Guest lounge. Day in OK. TV in rooms & guest lounge. Drying facilities. Bike storage. Walkers particularly welcome. Book-ahead service. Bunk room also avail. sleeps five, £12.50 pp incl. light b'fast, full cooked at extra cost. Self-catering cottage avail. sleeps 6.

Sheila & John Paisley
Kirkbeag
Kincraig, by KINGUSSIE, PH21 1ND
Tel/Fax: 01540 651298
email: kirkbeag@kincraig.com
web: www.kincraig.com/kirkbeag.htm
STB ★★★ B&B, Walkers Welcome

35 / NH 840068 Open all year. Rooms: 1T, 1D. £18.50 pp. Single occ. T/D: any time, £none - £5.00 extra. No ensuite. Bath avail. B'fast 8.00am - 8.30am, early b'fast from 7.00am by arr. Packed lunches by arr. Eve meal by arr. 7.00pm - 8.00pm, £10.00 - £12.00, bring your own drinks. Guest lounge. Day in OK. TV in guest lounge. Drying facilities. Bike storage. Walkers particularly welcome. Book-ahead service.

Mrs Sheena Brien
Ardinsh, The Brae
Kincraig, by KINGUSSIE
PH21 1NA
Tel: 01540 651726
email: asbrien@ardinsh.fsnet.co.uk

35 / NH 831057 Open Apr/May - Sep/Oct. Rooms: 1T, 1D. T: £18.00 pp D: £20.00 pp. Single occ. T/D: any time, no extra. Ensuite avail. with shower/bath. Bath avail. B'fast 7.00am - 9.00am, early b'fast from 6.30am by arr. Packed lunches by arr. Guest lounge. Day in OK. TV in TV lounge. No smoking. Bike storage. Book-ahead service.

Evening/bar meals:
– The Ossian Hotel *(see main entry)*

'Bath avail. all rooms' indicates that, if desired, a bath may be taken instead of a shower, and the availability does not depend on which room is occupied, though the bath may be a shared one.

Feshie Bridge (Inverness-shire)

Helen & Jim Gillies
Balcraggan House
Feshie Bridge, Kincraig
by KINGUSSIE
PH21 1NG
Tel: 01540 651488

35 / NH 848045 Open all year. Rooms: 1T, 1D. £25.00 pp. Single occ. T/D: any time, £10.00 extra. Both rooms ensuite with bath. Shower avail. B'fast 7.00am - 9.00am, early b'fast from 6.00am by arr. Packed lunches by arr. Eve meal by arr. 7.00pm - 8.30pm, £15.00, bring your own drinks. Guest lounge. TV in rooms. No smoking. Drying facilities. Bike storage. Walkers particularly welcome. Book-ahead service.

Evening/bar meals: see also Kincraig.

Lagganlia (Inverness-shire)

Caroline Hayes
March House Guest House, Lagganlia
Kincraig, by KINGUSSIE, PH21 1NG
Tel/Fax: 01540 651388
Mob: 07890 532150
email: caroline@
    marchhse01.freeserve.co.uk
web: www.kincraig.com/march
STB ★★★ Guest House
Walkers Welcome   Taste of Scotland

35 / NH 857039 Open all year, except 27th Oct - 27th Dec. Rooms: 2T, 2D, 2F. T/D: £22.00 - £25.00 pp F: £55.00 - £65.00 per room. Single occ. T/D: any time, £none - £5.00 extra. Ensuite avail. with shower/bath. Bath avail. depending on room occ. B'fast 8.00am - 9.00am, early b'fast from 7.00am by arr. Packed lunches by arr. Eve meal by arr. 7.00pm, £17.00, bring your own drinks. Guest lounge. Day in OK. No TV (unless desperate). No smoking. Drying facilities. Bike storage. Walkers particularly welcome. Book-ahead service.

Evening/bar meals: see also Kincraig.

Aviemore (Inverness-shire)

Jenny & Colin Wilkinson
Carn Mhor, The Shieling
AVIEMORE, PH22 1QD
Tel: 01479 811004
Mob: 07887 592270
email: carnmhor@
    bushinternet.com
or: info@carnmhor.co.uk
web: www.carnmhor.co.uk
STB ★★ B&B, Walkers Welcome
A real outdoor-enthusiasts place to stay.

36 / NH 895140   Open all year.   Rooms: 1S, 2T,* 1D, 2F. S/T/D: £18.00 - £20.00 pp   F: £55.00 per room (2 adults + 2 children). Single occ. T/D: off peak only, no extra. Ensuite avail. with shower/bath. Bath avail. depending on room occ. B'fast 8.00am - 9.00am, early b'fast by arr. Packed lunches by arr. Eve meal by arr. £12.00, bring your own drinks. Guest lounge. Day in OK by arr. TV in rooms. No smoking. Drying facilities. Bike storage. Book-ahead service. Reductions for longer stays. Free guest passes to local golf & country club: swimming, jacuzzi, sauna, gym, etc. *Twin rooms convert to triple or double if required. *Friendly welcome, good food. Recommended. AJ*

Margaret & Graham Hall
Kinapol Guest House, Dalfaber Road
AVIEMORE, PH22 1PY
Tel/Fax: 01479 810513
email: kinapol@aol.com
web: www.aviemore.co.uk/kinapol
STB ★★ Guest House

36 / NH 896123   Open all year. Rooms: 3D, 2F.*   From £15.00 pp. Single occ. T/D: off peak only, from £1.00 extra. No ensuite. Bath avail. B'fast 8.00am - 9.00am, early b'fast from 7.30pm by arr. Packed lunches by arr. Guest lounge. Day in OK. TV in rooms & guest lounge. No smoking. Drying facilities. Bike storage. Book-ahead service. *Family rooms also avail. as twin or double.

MacKenzies Highland Inn 125 Grampian Road AVIEMORE, PH22 1RL Tel: 01479 810672 Fax: 01479 810595 email: Mackhotel@aol.com STB ★★ Inn, Walkers Welcome	36 / NH 894129 Open all year. Rooms: 5T, 5D. £20.00 - £25.00 pp. Single occ. T/D: off peak only, £5.00 extra. Ensuite avail. with shower. Bath avail. depending on room occ. B'fast 8.00am - 9.30am, early b'fast from 7.30am by arr. Packed lunches by arr. Eve meals 4.00pm - 9.00pm. Full licence. Day in room OK. TV in rooms. Drying facilities. Bike storage. Book-ahead service.
Peter & Gail Conn Cairngorm Guest House, Grampian Road AVIEMORE, PH22 1RP Tel/Fax: 01479 810630 email: conns@lineone.net web: www.aviemore.co.uk /cairngormguesthouse STB ★★ Guest House Walkers Welcome AA ◆◆◆	36 / NH 895131 Open all year. Rooms: 3T, 5D, 2F. T: £18.00 - £24.00 pp D: £18.00 - £30.00 pp F: £15.00 - £23.00 pp. Single occ. T/D: off peak only, £10.00 - £20.00 extra. Ensuite avail. with shower. Bath avail. depending on room occ. B'fast 7.45am - 8.45am, early b'fast by arr. Packed lunches by arr. Guest lounge. Day in OK. TV in rooms & guest lounge. Drying facilities. Bike storage. Walkers particularly welcome. Book-ahead service.
Jill & Jonathan Gatenby Ravenscraig Guest House 141 Grampian Road AVIEMORE, PH22 1RP Tel: 01479 810278 Fax: 01479 812742 email: ravenscrg@aol.com web: www.aviemoreonline.com STB ★★ Guest House, Walkers Welcome AA ◆◆◆ RAC ◆◆◆	36 / NH 895131 Open all year. Rooms: 1S, 4T, 5D, 2F. £18.00 - £25.00 pp.* Single occ. T/D: any time, £none - £25.00 extra. All rooms ensuite with shower. No bath. B'fast 8.00am - 9.00am, early b'fast from 7.30am by arr. Packed lunches by arr. Guest lounge. Day in OK. TV in rooms & guest lounge. Drying facilities. Bike storage. Walkers particularly welcome. Book-ahead service. *Children in family room: half price.
Michael & Tracey Willies Ardlogie Guest House, Dalfaber Road AVIEMORE, PH22 1PU Tel: 01479 810747 email: ardlogie.aviemore@ lineone.net web: www.aviemore.co.uk/ardlogie STB ★★ Guest House Walkers Welcome	36 / NH 896122 Open all year. Rooms: 1T, 4D, 1F. T/D: £20.00 - £25.00 pp F: £40.00 - £60.00 per room. Single occ. T/D: any time, £5.00 extra. Ensuite avail. with shower. No bath. B'fast 8.00am - 8.45am, early b'fast from 7.00am by arr. Packed lunches by arr. Day in room OK. TV in rooms. No smoking. Drying facilities. Bike storage. Walkers particularly welcome. Book-ahead service. Free guest passes to local golf & country club: swimming, jacuzzi, sauna, gym, etc.

Evening/bar meals: plenty of choice in Aviemore, also:
- The Rowan Tree Country Hotel, Loch Alvie, by AVIEMORE, PH22 1QB   36 / NH 873095
   01479 810207 enquiries@rowantreehotel.com www.rowantreehotel.com
   Open all year except mid Nov - early Dec. Light refreshments 11.00am - 6.00pm.
   High teas 4.30pm - 5.45pm. Dinner 7.30pm for 8.00pm. B&B from around £30.00 pp.
   Booking essential for High Teas & Dinners. *Excellent food. Recommended. AJ*
Bike hire:
- Bothy Bikes, Unit 7, Aviemore Shopping Centre, Grampian Road, AVIEMORE
   PH22 1RH 01479 810111
Tourist info: Grampian Road, AVIEMORE, PH22 1PP 01479 810363 (All year)

Glenmore *(Inverness-shire)*

Mrs Mary Ferguson Cairn Eilrig, Glenmore AVIEMORE, PH22 1QU Tel: 01479 861223 email: mary@cairneilrig.fsnet.co.uk STB ★★★ B&B, Walkers Welcome	36 / NH 979097 Open all year. Rooms: 1T, 1F. From £17.00 pp.* Single occ. T/D: any time, £3.00 extra. No ensuite. Bath avail. B'fast 8.00am - 8.30am, early b'fast from 7.00am by arr. Packed lunches by arr. Guest lounge. Day in OK. TV in guest lounge. Drying facilities. Bike storage. Book-ahead service. *Children in family room: half price.

Evening/bar meals:
- Glenmore Lodge National Sports Centre, AVIEMORE, PH22 1QU   36 / NH 987094
  01479 861256   enquiries@glenmorelodge.org.uk   www.glenmorelodge.org.uk
  Bar meals 5.00pm - 7.00pm (Mon - Tue), 5.00pm - 9.00pm (Wed - Sun).

Teas etc:
- Glenmore Shop & Cafe, Glenmore, AVIEMORE, PH22 1QU 01479 861253   36 / NH 974098
  www.aviemore.co.uk/glenmoreski Open daily, 8.30am - 5.30pm (Sept - Jun),
  8.30am - 8.00pm (Jul - Aug).

Bike hire:
- Glenmore Mountain Bikes, Glenmore Shop, Glenmore, AVIEMORE, PH22 1QU
  01479 861253 (Day) 01479 841514 (Eve)

Loch Eil to Loch Mullardoch (Sections 10 & 11)

Inverie – Mallaig – Glenfinnan – Kinlocheil – South Laggan – Invergarry – Glenmoriston
Ault na Chruinn – Inverinate – Dornie – Ardelve – Glenelg – Arnisdale – Corran
For southern mountains see also Spean Bridge (Section 4)
For north-eastern mountains see Cannich (Sections 12 & 13)

Inverie *(Inverness-shire)*

Gwen Barrell & Murray Carden	33 / NG 767000 Open all year, except Nov, Jan, Feb. Rooms: 2T,
The Pier House, Inverie	1D, 1F. £40.00 pp incl. eve meal. Single occ. T/D: any time, no
Knoydart, by MALLAIG, PH41 4PL	extra. Ensuite avail. with shower. Bath avail. B'fast 8.00am -
Tel/Fax: 01687 462347	9.30am. Packed lunches by arr. Eve meals 6.30pm - 9.30pm.
email: eatandstay@thepierhouse.co.uk	Table licence. Day in OK. No TV. Drying facilities. Bike storage.
web: www.thepierhouse.co.uk	Walkers particularly welcome. Book-ahead service. 'Last Munro'
STB ★★ Restaurant with rooms	celebrations a speciality. Advance booking essential. Bike hire.
Taste of Scotland	Sells local books, maps, cards, artwork, midge repellent, etc.

Also self-catering accommodation and bunkhouse – for an accommodation list contact the Estate Office, Knoydart Foundation, Inverie, by Mallaig, Inverness-shire, PH41 4PL 01687 462242

Evening/bar meals:
– The Pier House Restaurant *(see main entry)*
– The Old Forge, Inverie, Knoydart, by MALLAIG, PH41 4PL 01687 462267   33 / NG 767000
info@theoldforge.co.uk www.theoldforge.co.uk Bar meals 6.30pm - 9.30pm.
First class food, looks very pretty, but I found not very filling. Recommended. AJ

Bike hire:
– Knoydart Bike Hire: contact The Pier House *(see main entry)*

Ferry service, Mallaig – Inverie:
– *TSMV Western Isles*, Bruce Watt Sea Cruises, Tel/Fax: 01687 462320
email: brucewattcruises@aol.com web: www.knoydart-ferry.co.uk
Sails Mon, Wed, Fri: depart Mallaig 10.15am, 2.15pm, depart Inverie 11.00am, 3.00pm.
From June to mid-September runs Mon - Fri (5 days).

Mallaig *(Inverness-shire)*

Mrs J. Watt	40 / NM 680971 Open Mar - Oct. Rooms: 2S, 2T, 1D, 1F.
Western Isles, East Bay	S: £20.00 pp T/D: £17.00 pp F: £50.00 per room. Single occ. T/D:
MALLAIG, PH41 4QG	off peak only, £3.00 extra. No ensuite. Bath avail. B'fast 7.30am -
Tel/Fax: 01687 462320	9.00am. Packed lunches by arr. Guest lounge. Day in OK. TV in
email: westrnisles@aol.com	rooms. No smoking. Drying facilities. Bike storage. Book-ahead
web: www.road-to-the-isles.org.uk	service.
/western-isles.html	*Mrs Watt's husband runs the Knoydart ferry service (see above), so*
STB ★★★ Guest House	*liaison over ferry arrangements is easy if you stay here. AJ*

'Bike storage' means that there is somewhere under cover for your bike, check at the time of booking if you need it to be securely lockable.

42

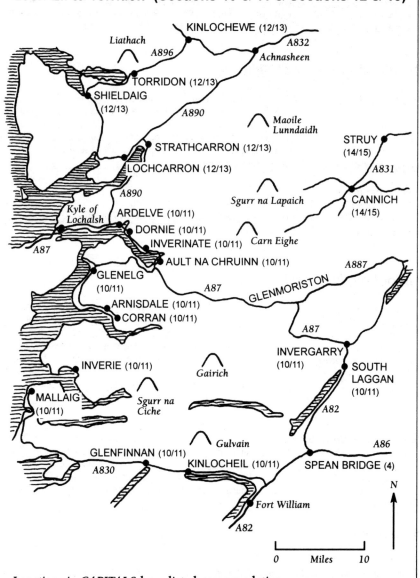

Loch Eil to Torridon (Sections 10 & 11 & Sections 12 & 13)

KINLOCHEWE (12/13)

Liathach

A896

A832

Achnasheen

TORRIDON (12/13)

SHIELDAIG (12/13)

A890

Maoile Lunndaidh

STRUY (14/15)

A831

STRATHCARRON (12/13)

LOCHCARRON (12/13)

Sgurr na Lapaich

CANNICH (14/15)

A890

Kyle of Lochalsh

ARDELVE (10/11)

DORNIE (10/11)

INVERINATE (10/11) *Carn Eighe*

A87

AULT NA CHRUINN (10/11)

A887

GLENELG (10/11)

A87

GLENMORISTON

ARNISDALE (10/11)

CORRAN (10/11)

A87

INVERGARRY (10/11)

SOUTH LAGGAN (10/11)

INVERIE (10/11)

Gairich

A86

MALLAIG (10/11)

Sgurr na Ciche

A82

GLENFINNAN (10/11)

Gulvain

A830

KINLOCHEIL (10/11)

SPEAN BRIDGE (4)

N

Fort William

A82

0   Miles   10

Locations in CAPITALS have listed accommodation

Mrs Christine King
Seaview, MALLAIG, PH41 4QS
Tel: 01687 462059 Fax: 01687 462768
email: seaviewmallaig@talk21.com
web: www.road-to-the-isles.org.uk/seaview.html
STB ★★ Guest House

40 / NM 676969 Open all year, except Dec. Rooms:
1T, 2D, 2F. T/D: £16.00 - £20.00 pp F: £18.00 pp.
Single occ. T/D: off peak only, £5.00 extra. Ensuite
avail. with shower. Bath avail. all rooms. B'fast
8.00am - 9.00am, early b'fast from 7.30am by arr.
Day in room OK. TV in rooms.

Glenfinnan *(Inverness-shire)*

Mr & Mrs G. Scott
Craigag Lodge
GLENFINNAN
PH37 4LT
Tel: 01397 722240
Friendly welcome and a good breakfast. Recommended. AJ

40 / NM 922798 Open Apr - Oct. Rooms: 1T, 1D, 1F. £15.00 - £20.00 pp.
Single occ. T/D: any time, £5.00 extra. No ensuite. Bath avail. B'fast
8.30am, early b'fast from 8.00am by arr. Packed lunches by arr. Eve meal by
arr. 7.30pm, £10.00, bring your own drinks. Guest lounge. TV in guest
lounge. No smoking. Drying facilities. Book-ahead service.

Evening/bar meals:
- The Prince's House, GLENFINNAN, PH37 4LT 01397 722246   40 / NM 896811
  princeshouse@glenfinnan.co.uk www.glenfinnan.co.uk Bar meals 7.00pm - 9.00pm.
  B&B from around £37.00 pp. *Excellent food. Recommended. AJ*

Kinlocheil *(Inverness-shire)*

Sheena & Keith Mace
Aladale, Kinlocheil
by FORT WILLIAM, PH33 7NP
Tel: 01397 722200
email: keithmacealadale@talk21.com
web: www.road-to-the-isles.org.uk
    /aladale.html
STB ★★★ B&B, Walkers Welcome

40 / NM 959794 Open all year, except Christmas/N.Year. Rooms:
1T, 1D, 1F. £15.50 - £17.50 pp. Single occ. T/D: any time, £none
- £7.50 extra. No ensuite. No bath, showers only. B'fast 8.00am -
9.00am, early b'fast from 7.00am by arr. Packed lunches by arr.
Eve meal by arr. off-peak season only, 7.00pm - 8.00pm, £10.00
(3 courses), bring your own drinks. Guest lounge. Day in OK. TV
in rooms. No smoking. Drying facilities. Bike storage. Walkers
particularly welcome. Book-ahead service.

Mrs F. A. Nisbet
Dailanna Guest House, Kinlocheil
by FORT WILLIAM, PH33 7NP
Tel/Fax: 01397 722253
email: flo@dailanna.co.uk
web: www.dailanna.co.uk
STB ★★★★ B&B

40 / NM 984789 Open Feb - Nov. Rooms: 2T, 1D, 1F.
T/D: £22.50 pp F: £60.00 per room. Single occ. T/D: off peak
only, no extra. All rooms ensuite with shower/bath. Bath avail.
depending on room occ. B'fast 8.30am, early b'fast by arr.
Packed lunches by arr. Guest lounge. Day in OK. TV in guest
lounge. Drying facilities. Limited bike storage. Book-ahead
service.

Evening/bar meals: see Glenfinnan

Prices quoted are subject to agreement at the time of booking, particularly with regard to single occupancy of a twin, double, or family room.

South Laggan (Inverness-shire)

Mrs Frances Jamieson	34 / NN 294972 Open all year. Rooms: 1T, 2D. £14.00 - £17.00 pp.
Lilac Cottage, South Laggan	Single occ. T/D: any time, £none - £5.00. No ensuite. Bath avail. B'fast
by SPEAN BRIDGE	8.00am - 9.00am, early b'fast from 7.00am by arr. Packed lunches by arr.
PH34 4EA	Eve meal by arr. 6.30pm - 7.00pm, £12.00, bring your own drinks. Guest
Tel: 01809 501410	lounge. Day in OK. TV in guest lounge. No smoking. Drying facilities.
email: lilac.cottage@virgin.net	Bike storage. Walkers particularly welcome. Book-ahead service.

Ian & Janet Shearer	34 / NN 291969 Open all year, except Christmas/N.Year.
Forest Lodge, South Laggan	Rooms: 2T, 2D, 3F. £18.00 - £22.00 pp. Single occ. T/D: any
by SPEAN BRIDGE, PH34 4EA	time, £7.00 extra. Ensuite avail. with shower. Bath avail.
Tel: 01809 501219 Fax: 01809 501476	depending on room occ. B'fast 8.30am - 9.00am, early b'fast
email: info@flgh.co.uk	by arr. Packed lunches by arr. Eve meal by arr. 7.30pm,
web: www.flgh.co.uk	£12.50, bring your own drinks. Guest lounge. Day in OK. TV
STB ★★★ Guest House	in guest lounge. No smoking. Drying facilities. Bike storage.
Walkers Welcome AA ◆◆◆	Book-ahead service.

Evening/bar meals:
- Letterfinlay Lodge Hotel, Loch Lochy, by SPEAN BRIDGE, PH34 4DZ   34 / NN 248911
  01397 712622 Bar meals 6.30pm - 8.00pm. B&B from around £35.00 pp.
- Great Glen Water Park, South Laggan, by SPEAN BRIDGE, PH34 4EA   34 / NN 303983
  01809 501381 *A la carte* restaurant 6.00pm - 8.30pm.

Invergarry (Inverness-shire)

Robert & Barbara Withers	34 / NH 291010 Open all year, except 24th/25th Dec. Rooms: 1S, 2T,
Craigard Guest House	5D. S: £21.00 pp T: £18.50 pp D: £18.50/£21.00 pp. Single occ. T/D:
INVERGARRY, PH35 4HG	any time, £5.00 extra. Ensuite avail. with shower/bath. Bath avail.
Tel: 01809 501258	depending on room occ. B'fast 8.00am - 8.30am, early b'fast from
email: bob@craigard.saltire.org	6.30am by arr. Packed lunches by arr. Eve meal by arr. 7.00pm,
web: www.craigard.saltire.org	£16.00. Residents licence. Guest lounge. TV in rooms & guest lounge.
AA ◆◆◆◆	No smoking. Drying facilities. Bike storage. Walkers particularly
	welcome. Book-ahead service.

This is one of my favourite places to stay – a friendly welcome and good food have made this a 'home from home'. Also the nearest B&B (apart from the Tomdoun Hotel) to Kinloch Hourn by road. Recommended. AJ

Mrs Janet Willison	34 / NH 310012 Open all year. Rooms: 1S, 1T, 1D, 1F. £15.00 pp.
1,2,3 Nursery Cottages	Single occ. T/D: off peak only, no extra. No ensuite. Bath avail.
INVERGARRY, PH35 4HL	B'fast 7.00am - 9.30am, early b'fast from 6.00am by arr. Packed
Tel/Fax: 01809 501285	lunches by arr. Eve meal by arr. 6.00pm - 8.00pm, £10.00, bring your
email: janet_willison@	own drinks. Lounge shared with hosts, avail. eve only. Day in room
hotmail.com	OK. TV in rooms. Drying facilities. Bike storage. Walkers
web: www.glengarryholidays	particularly welcome. Book-ahead service. Self-catering chalet avail.
.co.uk	sleeps 4.

It is assumed, and not stated in each entry, that everywhere will have at least a shower available for the use of guests.

Mrs Helen Fraser
Ardfriseal, Mandally
INVERGARRY, PH35 4HP
Tel: 01809 501281
email: fraser@ardfriseal.freeserve.co.uk

34 / NH 291005 Open May - Oct. Rooms: 1T, 2D. £16.00 - £17.00 pp. Single occ. T/D: off peak only, £5.00 extra. No ensuite. Bath avail. all rooms. B'fast 8.00am - 8.30am, early b'fast from 7.30am by arr. Guest lounge. TV in guest lounge. Limited drying facilities. Bike storage. Book-ahead service.

Mrs Marion Johnstone
Dunmar
INVERGARRY
PH35 4HP
Tel: 01809 501467

34 / NH 308008 Open Easter - Oct. Rooms: 2T, 1D. £14.00 pp. Single occ. T/D: any time, no extra. Ensuite avail. with shower. Bath avail. all rooms. B'fast 8.00am - 8.30am, early b'fast by arr. Guest lounge. Day in lounge OK. TV in one room & guest lounge. Drying facilities. Bike storage. Book-ahead service.

Evening/bar meals:
- Invergarry Hotel, INVERGARRY, PH35 4HJ 01809 501206   34 / NH 307011
  hotel@invergarry.net www.invergarry.net Bar meals 6.00pm - 9.00pm.
  B&B from around £35.00 pp. *Excellent food and real ale. Recommended. AJ*
Teas etc:
- Café at Invergarry Hotel, INVERGARRY, PH35 4HJ   34 / NH 307011
  Open daily, Easter - Oct, 10.00am - 7.00pm.

Glenmoriston *(Inverness-shire)*

Mrs G. McAdams
Ceannacroc Farm
Glenmoriston
INVERNESS
IV63 7YN
Tel: 01320 340236

34 / NH 228113 Open all year.* Rooms: 3T, 4D. £16.00 - £19.00 pp. Single occ. T/D: any time, £2.00 extra. Ensuite avail. with shower. Bath avail. all rooms. B'fast 8.00am - 9.00am, early b'fast by arr. Packed lunches by arr. Eve meal by arr. 6.00pm - 8.00pm, £5.00 - £10.00, bring your own drinks. Guest lounge. TV in guest lounge. Drying facilities. Bike storage. Book-ahead service. *Except own holidays.

Cluanie Inn, Glenmoriston
INVERNESS, IV63 7YW
Tel: 01320 340238
Fax: 01320 340293
email: cluanie@ecosse.net
web: www.cluanie.co.uk
STB ★★ Inn
AA ★★ RAC ★★

33 / NH 076117 Open all year. Rooms: 2S, 4T, 6D, 3F. S: £39.50 pp T: from £43.50 pp   D: from £39.50 pp   F: from £43.50 pp (2 people) + £19.50 pp (2 bunks). Single occ. T/D: off-peak only, £10.00 extra. Ensuite avail. with shower/bath. Bath avail. depending on room occ. B'fast 8.00am - 9.00am.* Packed lunches by arr. Eve meals 6.00pm - 8.30pm (limited food menu avail. all day). Full licence. Guest lounge. Day in OK. No TV (no reception).** Drying facilities. Bike storage. Walkers particularly welcome. Book-ahead service. *Cold tray b'fast avail. earlier. **Video units in all rooms & extensive video library avail. Also Clubhouse (twin or bunk bed rooms)

£25.50/£29.50 pp. Off-peak special offers for longer stays (Nov - Apr). Free Land Rover service by arr. to drop off guests in Glen Shiel, or help relocate to your own car. *Excellent food, open fire in winter, everything you need under one roof, and a fantastic location for the hills. Recommended. AJ*

Evening/bar meals:
- Cluanie Inn *(see main entry)*

Please read the entries in conjunction with the notes on pages 5 & 6.

Ault na Chruinn (Ross-shire)

Celia Munro
Glomach House, Ault na Chruinn
Glenshiel, by KYLE, IV40 8HN
Tel: 01599 511222 Fax: 01599 511382
email: glomachhouse@hotmail.com
web: www.glomach.co.uk
STB ★★★★ B&B

33 / NG 946204 Open all year. Rooms: 1T, 2D. £20.00 - £25.00 pp. Single occ. T/D: off peak only, £5.00 - £10.00 extra. All rooms ensuite with shower/bath. Bath avail. depending on room occ. B'fast 8.30am, early b'fast by arr. Guest lounge. TV in rooms & guest lounge. No smoking. Drying facilities. Bike storage. Walkers particularly welcome.

Evening/bar meals:
- Kintail Lodge Hotel, Glenshiel, by KYLE, IV40 8HL 01599 511275   33 / NG 938196
  kintaillodgehotel@btinternet.com www.kintaillodgehotel.co.uk Bar meals 6.00pm - 9.30pm.
  B&B from around £30.00 pp.
Taxi service: (if you don't want to walk all the way back up Glen Shiel)
- Kyle Taxi Company 01599 534323

Inverinate (Ross-shire)

Berwyn & Beryl Edwards
Aveley, Inverinate
by KYLE, IV40 8HB
Tel: 01599 511200

33 / NG 911224 Open all year. Rooms: 1T, 2D. £15.00 pp. Single occ. T/D: any time, no extra. No ensuite. Bath avail. B'fast 7.00am - 9.00am, early b'fast from 6.00am by arr. Packed lunches by arr. Guest lounge. Day in OK. TV in guest lounge. Drying facilities. Bike storage. Book-ahead service.

Mr & Mrs J. Mackinnon
Cala-Reidh, Inverinate
by KYLE, IV40 8HF
Tel: 01599 511353

33 / NG 936210 Open Easter - Oct. Rooms: 1T, 1D, 1F. £15.00 pp. Single occ. T/D: any time, £1.00 extra. No ensuite. Bath avail. B'fast 8.00am - 9.30am, early b'fast from 7.30 by arr. Packed lunches by arr. Guest lounge. TV in guest lounge. No smoking. Drying facilities. Bike storage. Book-ahead service.

Possibly the best-appointed breakfast table in the Highlands. Recommended. AJ

Mrs Jane Croy
Mo-Dhachaidh, Inverinate
by KYLE, IV40 8HB
Tel: 01599 511351
email: davidjanecroy@
         talk21.com
STB ★★★ B&B

33 / NG 908229 Open all year. Rooms: 1S, 1T, 1D, 1F. S: £20.00 - £22.00 pp   T/D: £17.00 - £20.00 pp   F: £50.00 - £60.00 per room. Single occ. T/D: any time, no extra. Ensuite avail. with shower. No bath. B'fast 7.00am - 9.00am, early b'fast from 6.00am by arr. Packed lunches by arr. Guest lounge. Day in OK. TV in guest lounge. No smoking. Drying facilities. Bike storage. Book-ahead service.

Mrs J. A. Fraser
Cruachan, 5 Glebe Road
Inverinate, by KYLE, IV40 8HD
Tel: 01599 511328
STB ★★ B&B

33 / NG 928213 Open all year. Rooms: 2F. £16.00 pp. Single occ. any time, £4.00 extra. No ensuite. Bath avail. both rooms. B'fast 8.00am - 9.00am, early b'fast from 7.30am by arr. Packed lunches by arr. Guest lounge. TV in guest lounge. Drying facilities. Book-ahead service.

Evening/bar meals: see Dornie

Many proprietors will provide a continental/cold/tray/packed/DIY breakfast if you need it earlier than their stated earliest time.

Dornie (Ross-shire)

Mrs D. Bryson
Rock House, Dornie
by KYLE, IV40 8DX
Tel/Fax: 01599 555387
email: jbryson@talk21.com
STB ★★★ B&B

33 / NG 882264   Open all year.   Rooms: 1T, 2D.   £17.50 - £22.50 pp.   Single occ. T/D: off peak only, £5.00 extra. Ensuite avail. with shower/bath. Bath avail. depending on room occ. B'fast 8.30am - 9.00am, early b'fast from 7.15am by arr. Day in room OK. TV in rooms. No smoking. Drying facilities. Bike storage.

Mrs Gordon Canning
Tigh Tasgaidh, Francis Street
Dornie, by KYLE, IV40 8EJ
Tel: 01599 555242
email: lgordoncan@aol.com
web: www.milford.co.uk
/scotland/accom/h-a-1828.html
STB ★★★ B&B, Walkers Welcome

33 / NG 882265   Open all year.   Rooms: 1S, 1T, 1D.   £23.00 - £25.00 pp.   Single occ. T/D: any time, no extra. Ensuite avail. with shower.   Bath avail.   B'fast 7.30am - 8.45am, early b'fast from 6.45am by arr. Packed lunches by arr. Guest lounge. Day in OK. TV in rooms.   No smoking.   Drying facilities.   Bike storage. Walkers particularly welcome. Book-ahead service. Car drop-offs in morning for Five Sisters, etc. donation to charity. Self-catering accommodation avail. sleeps 4.

Evening/bar meals:
– Dornie Hotel, Francis Street, Dornie, by KYLE, IV40 8DT 01599 555205   33 / NG 882265
  dornie@masadafish.com Bar meals 6.00pm - 9.00pm. B&B from around £35.00 pp.
  The reputation of the Dornie Hotel's superb food goes far across the Highlands, and is one I
  entirely endorse. An extensive menu, with the same choice in the restaurant or bar. And on a
  clear day you can see Blaven from the bar window... Recommended. AJ

Ardelve (Ross-shire)

Mrs Phyllis Peterkin
Sealladh Mara, Ardelve
by KYLE, IV40 8EY
Tel: 01599 555296
Fax: 01599 555250
STB ★★★ B&B

33 / NG 871269   Open all year.   Rooms: 1T, 3D.   T: £16.00 pp D: £16.00/£20.00 pp.   Single occ. T/D: any time, £4.00 extra. Ensuite avail. with shower. Bath avail. B'fast 8.00am - 8.30am, early b'fast by arr. Packed lunches by arr. Guest lounge. Day in OK. TV in rooms & guest lounge. Drying facilities. Book-ahead service.

Paul & Sheena Newton
Caberfeidh House, Ardelve
by KYLE, IV40 8DY
Tel: 01599 555293
email: info@caberfeidh.plus.com
web: www.caberfeidh.plus.com
STB ★★ Guest House

33 / NG 876268   Open all year.   Rooms: 1S, 2T, 3D.   S: £20.00 pp T: £18.00 - £20.00 pp D: £18.00 - £22.00 pp.   Single occ. T/D: off peak only, about £10.00 extra. Ensuite avail. with shower. No bath. B'fast 8.00am - 9.00am, early b'fast from 7.30am by arr.   Packed lunches by arr. Guest lounge. Day in OK. TV in rooms & guest lounge. No smoking. Drying facilities. Bike storage. Book-ahead service.

Evening/bar meals: see Dornie

'Day in OK' means that you may stay in your room (or guest lounge, if available) during the day, but this does not apply on your day of arrival or departure, and access to service the room must be allowed at some time.

Glenelg (Inverness-shire

Mary Chisholm Galder, Glenelg by KYLE, IV40 8JZ Tel: 01599 522287 STB ★★★ B&B	33 / NG 809203 Open all year. Rooms: 1S, 1T, 2D. S: £15.00 - £20.00 pp T/D: £18.00 - £22.00 pp. Single occ. T/D: any time, £3.00 extra. Ensuite avail. with shower. Bath avail. B'fast 8.00am - 10.00am, early b'fast by arr. Packed lunches by arr. Eve meal by arr. 6.00pm - 8.00pm, bring your own drinks. Guest lounge. Day in OK by arr. TV in guest lounge. Drying facilities. Bike storage. Book-ahead service.

A warm welcome, good food, and the most comfortable bed I've slept in. Recommended. AJ

Mrs Margaret Cameron Marabhaig 7 Coulindoune Glenelg, by KYLE IV40 8JU Tel: 01599 522327	33 / NG 807188 Open Jan - Nov. Rooms: 2T, 3D. T: £18.00 pp D: £19.00 pp. Single occ. T/D: any time, £2.00 extra. Ensuite avail. with shower. Bath avail. B'fast 7.00am - 9.00am, early b'fast from 6.00am by arr. Packed lunches by arr. Eve meal by arr. 6.00pm - 9.00pm, £12.00. Guest lounge. Day in OK. TV in rooms & guest lounge. No smoking. Drying facilities. Bike storage. Book-ahead service.

Evening/bar meals:
- Glenelg Inn, Glenelg, by KYLE, IV40 8JR 01599 522273   33 / NG 813193
  Bar meals 6.00pm - 9.00pm. DB&B from around £79.00 pp.
  I found a very limited and unappealing selection of bar meals here, and my enquiry about food was given a sarcastic response from the person behind the bar. I can't really recommend eating here, but it is a long way to go to find anywhere else. AJ

Arnisdale (Inverness-shire

o 788 v 576 674 BARSSALE phyllis & stan

Mr & Mrs L. Morrison Croftfoot, Arnisdale by KYLE, IV40 8JL Tel: 01599 522352 email: croftfoot@ themail.co.uk	33 / NG 843105 Open Mar - Oct. Rooms: 1T, 1F. £19.00 pp. Single occ. T/D: any time, no extra. No ensuite. Bath avail. B'fast 7.30am - 8.30am, early b'fast from 6.30am by arr. Packed lunches by arr. Eve meal by arr. 6.30pm - 8.00pm, £16.00, bring your own drinks. Lounge shared with hosts. Day in OK. TV in shared lounge. Drying facilities. Walkers particularly welcome. Book-ahead service.

Len Morrison also operates a boat service by prior arrangement across Loch Hourn to drop off at or pick up from Barrisdale, etc. Ring for rates and to check availability (may depend on weather). AJ

Evening/bar meals: see also Glenelg

Corran (Inverness-shire)

Sheena Nash Corran, Arnisdale by KYLE IV40 8JH Tel: 01599 522336	33 / NG 849092 Open all year. Rooms: 1S, 1T, 1D, 1F. £14.00 pp. Single occ. T/D: any time, £3.00 extra. No ensuite. Bath avail. B'fast 8.00am - 9.30am, early b'fast from 7.00am by arr. Packed lunches by arr. Eve meal by arr. 6.00pm - 8.00pm, £20.00, bring your own drinks. Guest lounge. Day in OK. TV in rooms & guest lounge. Drying facilities. Bike storage. Walkers particularly welcome. Book-ahead service.

Evening/bar meals: see also Glenelg
Teas etc:
- Sheena's Tea Hut, Corran *(adjacent to B&B – see main entry)*

01456 4152 63 Brudtowe

Loch Mullardoch to Torridon (Sections 12 & 13)

Cannich – Struy – Strathcarron – Lochcarron – Shieldaig – Torridon
For Torridon mountains see also Kinlochewe (Sections 14 & 15)

Cannich (Inverness-shire)

Stephen Bassett & Gill Kirkpatrick
Kerrow House, Cannich
by BEAULY, IV4 7NA
Tel: 01456 415243 Fax: 01456 415425
email: stephen@
    kerrow-house.demon.co.uk
web: www.kerrow-house.demon.co.uk
STB ★★★ B&B, Walkers welcome

26 / NH 330306   Open all year.   Rooms: 1T, 2D, 1F.
T: £22.00 - £28.00 pp   D: £22.00 - £32.00 pp   F: £20.00 - £28.00 pp.   Single occ. T/D: any time, £none - £10.00 extra. Ensuite avail.   B'fast 8.30am, early b'fast from 8.00am by arr. Packed lunches by arr.   Residents licence.   Guest lounge.   TV in rooms.   No smoking.   Drying facilities.   Bike storage. Walkers particularly welcome.

George & Ishbel Strachan
Upper Glassburn House
Cannich, by BEAULY, IV4 7LE
Tel: 01456 415217
email: ishbel.strachan@
    virgin.net

26 / NH 368343 Open all year. Rooms: 1S, 1T, 2D. £17.00 pp. Single occ. T/D: any time, no extra. No ensuite. Bath avail. B'fast 7.00am - 9.00am, early b'fast any time by arr. Packed lunches by arr. Eve meal by arr. 7.00pm - 8.00pm, £13.00, bring your own drinks. Guest lounge. Day in OK. TV in guest lounge. Drying facilities. Bike storage. Book-ahead service.

Ian & Jane Mure
Comar Lodge, Cannich
by BEAULY, IV4 7NB
Tel/Fax: 01456 415251
Mob: 07769 705998
email: IanMure@aol.com
web: www.comarlodge.co.uk

26 / NH 332313 Open all year. Rooms: 2T, 1D. £20.00 - £24.00 pp. Single occ. T/D: any time, £10.00 - £15.00 extra. Ensuite avail. with shower. Bath avail. B'fast 7.00am - 9.00am. Packed lunches by arr. Eve meal by arr. 7.30pm - 8.00pm, £15.00, bring your own wine. TV in rooms. No smoking. Drying facilities. Bike storage. Walkers particularly welcome. Book-ahead service. Bike hire avail.

Mrs L. M. Ferguson
Westward Guest House
Cannich, by BEAULY
IV4 7LT
Tel: 01456 415225
Pleasant welcome and a good breakfast. Recommended. AJ

26 / NH 337317 Open Mar - Dec. Rooms: 1S, 3T. £18.00 pp. Single occ. T/D: any time, no extra. Ensuite avail. with shower. No bath. B'fast 7.00am - 10.00am. Packed lunches by arr. Guest lounge. Day in OK. TV in guest lounge. Drying facilities. Bike storage. Walkers particularly welcome. Book-ahead service.

Evening/bar meals:
 – Slaters Arms, Cannich, by BEAULY, IV4 7LN 01456 415215   26 / NH 335316
   Bar meals 6.00pm - 10.00pm. *Good unpretentious food. Recommended. AJ*
Bike hire:
 – Comar Lodge *(see main entry)*

'Walkers particularly welcome' indicates that the proprietors have rated themselves as making specific efforts to cater for the needs of guests who are walkers; if this is not stated in an entry, then walkers are just as much welcome as any other guest.

Struy *(Inverness-shire)*

Douglas Brown
Glass Restaurant, Struy
by BEAULY, IV4 7JS
Tel: 01463 761219
email: glassrest@supanet.com
web: *under development*

26 / NH 401400   Open 20th Mar - 26th Dec.   Rooms: 4D.   £18.00 pp. Single occ. T/D: any time, no extra. Ensuite avail. with bath. Bath avail. B'fast 8.00am - 9.00am, early b'fast from 7.30am by arr. Packed lunches by arr. Meals 12.00noon - 9.00pm, £17.95. Full licence. Guest lounge. Day in OK. TV in rooms. Drying facilities. Bike storage. Book-ahead service. Advance booking essential in restaurant for non-residents.

I haven't stayed here, but I had the best steak I've ever eaten (and I've had more than a few) in the restaurant. Recommended. AJ

Strathcarron *(Ross-shire)*

Jim & Jennifer Levy
The Shieling, Achintee
STRATHCARRON
IV54 8YX
Tel: 01520 722364

25 / NG 942417   Open all year.   Rooms: 1S, 2T.   S: £18.00 pp   T: £20.00 pp. Single occ. T/D: off peak only, no extra. Ensuite avail. with shower. Bath avail. B'fast 7.00am - 8.30am, early b'fast from 6.00am by arr. Packed lunches by arr. Eve meal by arr. Oct - Mar only, £12.00, bring your own wine. Guest lounge. Day in OK. TV in guest lounge. No smoking. Drying facilities. Bike storage. Walkers particularly welcome. Book-ahead service.

I haven't stayed here, but the welcome I received when I called in means I would very much like to. Recommended. AJ

Evening/bar meals:
– Strathcarron Hotel, STRATHCARRON, IV54 8YR 01520 722227   25 / NG 941422
Bar meals all day until 9.00pm. B&B from around £30.00 pp.

Lochcarron *(Ross-shire)*

Ms Moyra Innes
Aultsigh, Croft Road, Lochcarron
STRATHCARRON, IV54 8YA
Tel: 01520 722558
email: moyra.innes@talk21.com
web: www.wester-ross.com
/accommodation/aultsigh.htm

25 / NG 901398   Open all year, except Christmas/N.Year.   Rooms: 1T, 1D, 1F.   £17.00 - £18.00 pp.* Single occ. T/D: any time, £none - £8.00 extra. No ensuite. Bath avail. B'fast 8.00am - 8.30am, early b'fast from 7.00am by arr. Packed lunches by arr. Guest lounge. Day in OK. TV in guest lounge. Drying facilities. Bike storage. Book-ahead service. *Children in family room: usually half price.

Mrs C. Michael
Castle Cottage
Main Street, Lochcarron
STRATHCARRON, IV54 8YB
Tel: 01520 722564
STB ★★★ B&B

25 / NG 907400   Open all year.   Rooms: 2T, 1D.   T: £18.00 pp D: £20.00 - £22.00 pp. Single occ. T/D: off peak only, £none - £7.00 extra. Ensuite avail. with shower. Bath avail. B'fast 8.00am - 9.00am, early b'fast from 7.30am by arr. Guest lounge. Day in OK. TV in guest lounge. Drying facilities. Bike storage. Book-ahead service.

'Book-ahead service' means that the proprietors are willing to make a phone booking for you if you wish to move on to another establishment listed in the Guide; but you should agree the exact terms of the service at the time of request.

Mrs Jean Davidson
Rockview, Main Street
Lochcarron
STRATHCARRON, IV54 8YD
Tel: 01520 722526

25 / NG 902398 Open Easter - Oct. Rooms: 1S, 1F. £17.00 pp. Single occ. F: off peak only, £3.00 extra. No ensuite. Bath avail. both rooms. B'fast 7.45am - 8.30am, early b'fast from 7.15am by arr. Packed lunches by arr. Guest lounge (conservatory). Day in OK. TV in F room. Limited drying facilities. Book-ahead service.

Evening/bar meals:
- Lochcarron Hotel, Main Street, Lochcarron, STRATHCARRON, IV54 8YS   25 / NG 909402
  01520 722226 Bar meals 6.00pm - 9.00pm. B&B from around £33.00 pp.

Teas etc:
- Waterside Café, Main Street, Lochcarron, STRATHCARRON, IV54 8YD   25 / NG 902398
  01520 722303 Open daily, Easter - Oct, 8.30am - 7.30pm (Mon - Sat), 10.00am - 6.00pm (Sun); open Thurs, Fri, Sat, Nov - Easter, 9.30am - 7.00pm. Refreshments, snacks, & hot meals.

Tourist info: Main Street, Lochcarron, STRATHCARRON, IV54 8YB 01520 722357 (Apr - Oct)

Shieldaig *(Ross-shire)*

Trevor Bradley
Rowan Bank, Shieldaig
by STRATHCARRON
IV54 8XN
Tel: 01520 755246
web: www.wester-ross.com
       /accommodation
       /rowanbank.htm

24 / NG 817541 Open all year, except Christmas/N.Year.* Rooms: 1T, 1D, 1F. £20.00 pp.** Single occ. T/D: any time, £4.00 extra. All rooms ensuite with shower. No bath. B'fast 7.30am - 9.00am, early b'fast may be negotiable by arr. Eve meal by arr. until 7.30pm, but not every evening, bring your own drinks. Guest lounge. Day in OK. TV in guest lounge. No smoking. Drying facilities. Bike storage. Book-ahead service. Hillwalking proprietor, collection of walking books etc. in guest lounge. *May close for own holidays. **Reductions for longer stays except single occ. T/D; reductions for children.

Mrs M. Calcott
Tigh Fada, 117 Doire Aonar
nr Shieldaig
by STRATHCARRON, IV54 8XR
Tel/Fax: 01520 755248
STB ★★ B&B

24 / NG 806533 Open Feb - Nov. Rooms: 1T, 1F. £15.00 pp. Single occ. T/D: any time, no extra. No ensuite. Bath avail. B'fast 6.30am - 8.45am, early b'fast any time by arr. Packed lunches by arr. Eve meal by arr. 7.00pm, £8.50, bring your own drinks. Guest lounge. TV in guest lounge. No smoking. Drying facilities. Bike storage. Book-ahead service. Self-catering caravan and bungalow avail.

Marilyn & Tom Taylor
Rivendell Guest House, Shieldaig
by STRATHCARRON, IV54 8XN
Tel: 01520 755250
email: rivendell@wester-ross-net.co.uk
web: www.wester-ross.com
       /accommodation/rivendell.htm

24 / NG 814537 Open all year. Rooms: 3S, 3T, 6D. £18.50 pp. Single occ. T/D: any time, no extra. Ensuite avail. with shower. No bath. B'fast any time by arr. Packed lunch by arr. Eve meal 6.00pm - 8.00pm, £13.50, bring your own drinks. Guest lounge. Day in OK. TV avail. some rooms. No smoking. Drying facilities. Bike storage. Book-ahead service.

Very hospitable welcome, and a good breakfast. Recommended. AJ

Evening/bar meals:
- Shieldaig Bar at the Tigh an Eilean Hotel, Shieldaig, by STRATHCARRON   · · 24 / NG 815538
  IV54 8XN 01520 755251 Bar meals 6.00pm - 8.30pm. B&B from around £55.00 pp.

If a B&B states 'Open all year', the proprietors may close to take a holiday sometime themselves.

Torridon *(Ross-shire)*

Anne Thorburn	25 / NG 903550 Open May - Oct. Rooms: 1T, 1D. £18.00 pp.
Cronan, Newton, Torridon	Single occ. T/D: any time, no extra. No ensuite. Bath avail.
by ACHNASHEEN, IV22 2EZ	B'fast 8.00am - 8.30am, early b'fast from 7.00am by arr. Packed
Tel: 01445 791313	lunches by arr. Guest lounge. Day in OK. TV in guest lounge.
email: Kenneth.Thorburn@	Drying facilities. Bike storage. Walkers particularly welcome.
tinyworld.co.uk	Book-ahead service.

Evening/bar meals: see Shieldaig

Competition No. 1

To occupy yourselves while waiting for your evening meal...

Name the two Munros in the illustration on the front cover of this Guide. (Note that the illustrator has used a little artistic licence in the depiction. His artistic licence has been inspected, and it is valid and without endorsements.) Also give the name of the boat on which the compiler was standing when he took the photo on which the illustration was based. (A little lateral thinking should get you there.)

RULES. Please send your answers, name, and address, on a picture postcard of your home town (or your nearest locality of which picture postcards are available) to the publishers at the address on the back of the title page, by 1st July 2003. All entrants must be over 18 years of age; maximum one entry per person; no purchase necessary. In the event of any dispute, the compiler's decision is final. So that local knowledge does not give an unfair advantage, this competition is not open to anyone whose normal place of residence is within 100 miles (by direct line) of the mountains depicted.

PRIZES. The winner will be determined by drawing one entry out of a suitable receptacle containing all correct entries received by the closing date (or by an approximately equivalent pseudo-randomising selection process), and will be sent a bottle of Bells 8-year old scotch whisky. The next five correct entries drawn will each be sent a runners-up prize of a miniature of scotch whisky.

ANSWERS. The correct answers will be published on the publishers' web site after the closing date, with the names of the winner and runners-up. If no correct answers are received by the closing date, an extension period for entries may be announced on the web site.

Loch Maree to Ben Wyvis (Sections 14 & 15)

Kinlochewe – Achanalt – Lochluichart – Garve – Aultguish – Camusnagaul

Kinlochewe *(Ross-shire)*

Tom & Liz Forrest
Cromasaig, Torridon Road
Kinlochewe
by ACHNASHEEN, IV22 2PE
Tel: 01445 760234 Fax: 01445 760333
email: cromasaig@msn.com
web: www.cromasaig.com
STB ★★★ B&B, Walkers Welcome

19 / NH 024607 Open all year. Rooms: 1T, 1D, 1F. £20.00 pp. Single occ. T/D: any time, no extra. No ensuite, but all rooms private facilities with shower. No bath. B'fast 7.00am - 9.00am, early b'fast by arr. Packed lunches by arr. Eve meal by arr. 8.00pm, £13.00, bring your own drinks. Guest lounge. Day in OK. No TV. No smoking. Drying facilities. Bike storage. Walkers particularly welcome. Book-ahead service. Hillwalking proprietors. Sauna avail.

Lilah & David Ford
Hillhaven, Kinlochewe
by ACHNASHEEN, IV22 2PA
Tel: 01445 760204
email: hillhaven@
    kinlochewe.info
web: www.kinlochewe.info

19 / NH 026622 Open all year. Rooms: 1T, 2D. £22.50 pp. Single occ. T/D: any time, £2.50 extra. All rooms ensuite with shower. No bath. B'fast 7.45am - 8.30am, early b'fast from 6.00am by arr. Packed lunches by arr. Eve meal by arr. 6.30pm - 8.00pm, £12.00 - £15.00, bring your own drinks. Guest lounge. Day in OK. TV in guest lounge. No smoking. Drying facilities. Bike storage. Walkers particularly welcome. Book-ahead service. Members of HOST.

Kinlochewe Hotel & Bunkhouse
Kinlochewe
by ACHNASHEEN, IV22 2PA
Tel: 01445 760253
email: kinlochewehotel@
    tinyworld.co.uk
web: www.torridon-mountains.com
    /hotel/index.htm
STB ★ Small Hotel

19 / NH 028619 Open all year. Rooms: 2S, 4T, 3D, 1F. £22.50 - £25.00 pp.* Single occ. T/D: any time, extra depends on time of year. Ensuite avail. with shower/bath. Bath avail. B'fast 8.00am - 9.30am, early b'fast from 7.30am by arr. Packed lunches by arr. Eve meals 6.30pm - 8.30pm. Full licence. Guest lounge. Day in OK. TV in guest lounge. Drying facilities. Bike storage. Walkers particularly welcome. Book-ahead service. Bunkhouse also avail. with full kitchen facilities, £8.00 pp incl. showers, heating. *Children in family room: rates according to age.

Evening/bar meals:
– Kinlochewe Hotel *(see main entry)*

Achanalt *(Ross-shire)*

Donald & Sandra Northwood
Achanalt House, Achanalt
by GARVE, IV23 2QD
Tel: 01997 414366

20 / NH 260615 Open Apr - Sep. Rooms: 2D. £19.50 pp. Single occ. T/D: off peak only, £5.50 extra. Both rooms ensuite with shower. No bath. B'fast 7.30am - 9.00am, early b'fast by arr. Packed lunches by arr. Eve meal by arr. 7.00pm - 9.00pm. Table licence. Day in room OK. TV in rooms. No smoking. Drying facilities. Bike storage. Book-ahead service.

Teas etc:
– Achanalt House *(see main entry)*. Tea room open daily, Apr - Sep, 8.30am - 7.00pm, refreshments, snacks, light meals.

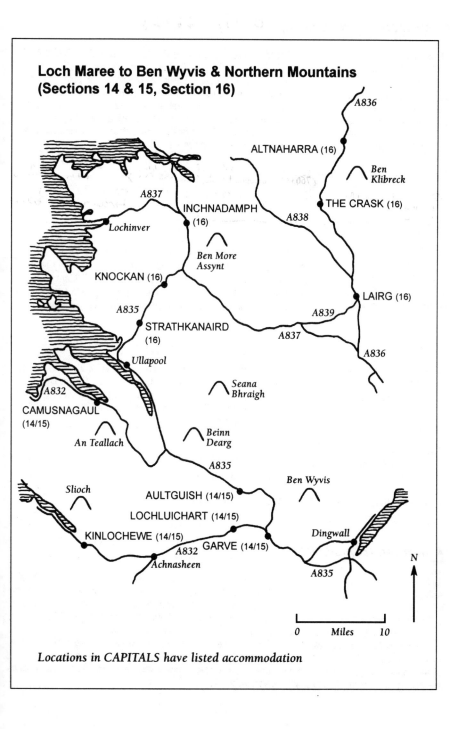

Loch Maree to Ben Wyvis & Northern Mountains
(Sections 14 & 15, Section 16)

A836

ALTNAHARRA (16)

Ben
Klibreck

A837

INCHNADAMPH
(16)

THE CRASK (16)

Lochinver

A838

Ben More
Assynt

KNOCKAN (16)

LAIRG (16)

A835

A839

STRATHKANAIRD
(16)

A837

A836

Ullapool

Seana
Bhraigh

A832

CAMUSNAGAUL
(14/15)

Beinn
Dearg

An Teallach

A835

Ben Wyvis

Slioch

AULTGUISH (14/15)

LOCHLUICHART (14/15)

Dingwall

KINLOCHEWE (14/15)

A832 GARVE (14/15)

Achnasheen

A835

N

0   Miles   10

Locations in CAPITALS have listed accommodation

Lochluichart (Ross-shire)

[handwritten: Inchlay Lodge 01997 455269]

Mr & Mrs S. Doyle 4 Mossford Cottages Lochluichart by GARVE, IV23 2QA Tel: 01997 414334 email: sealochluichart@cs.com web: *under development* STB ★★★ B&B	20 / NH 329631 Open all year. 1S, 1T, 1D, 1F. S/T/D: £15.00 - £18.00 pp F: £50.00 - £60.00 per room. Single occ. T/D: off peak only, £5.00 - £7.00 extra. Ensuite avail. with shower/bath. Bath avail. B'fast 8.00am - 9.00am, early b'fast from 6.30am by arr. Packed lunches by arr. Eve meal by arr. 6.30pm - 7.30pm, £10.00 (3 courses), bring your own drinks. Guest lounge. Day in OK. No TV. No smoking. Drying facilities. Bike storage. Walkers particularly welcome. Book-ahead service.

Evening/bar meals: see also Garve

[handwritten annotations: Birch Cottage — GARVE — Ray Clark 414 237 Brew your own beer etc]

Garve (Ross-shire)

Jean & Pete Hollingdale The Old Manse GARVE, IV23 2PX Tel/Fax: 01997 414201 email: petehollingdale@ supanet.com	20 / NH 387624 Open all year, except Christmas. Rooms: 1T, 2D. T: £16.50 pp D: £16.50 - £17.50 pp. Single occ. T/D: any time, no extra. Ensuite avail. with shower. Bath avail. B'fast 8.30am - 9.00am, early b'fast from 6.00am by arr. Guest lounge. Day in OK. No TV. No smoking. Drying facilities. Bike storage. Book-ahead service.
Bridget & Keith Frost Hazelbrae House GARVE, IV23 2PX Tel: 01997 414382 Mob: 07808 444937 email: bridgetandkeithfrost@ ntlworld.com web: www.highlandwelcome.co.uk	20 / NH 391621 Open all year. Rooms: 2T, 3D. £15.00 - £18.00 pp. Single occ. T/D: any time, no extra. No ensuite. Bath avail. B'fast 7.00am - 9.30am, early b'fast by arr. Packed lunches by arr. Guest lounge. Day in OK. TV in rooms & guest lounge. Bike storage. Walkers particularly welcome. Book-ahead service. Small kitchenette avail. for self-catering.

Evening/bar meals:
- The Garve Country Hotel, GARVE, IV23 2PR 01997 414205   20 / NH 394617
  Bar meals 6.30pm - 8.30pm. B&B from around £25.00 pp.

Bike hire:
- Seaforth Highland Country Estate, Brahan, DINGWALL, IV7 8EE 01349 861150

Aultguish (Ross-shire)

Richard & Lesley Sys Aultguish Inn by GARVE, IV23 2PQ Tel: 01997 455254 email: richard@rsys.freeserve.co.uk *or:* richard@aultguish.co.uk web: www.aultguish.co.uk	20 / NH 351704 Open all year. Rooms: 4S, 7T, 6D, 3F. £10.00 - £13.00 pp. Single occ. T/D: off peak only & if not busy, no extra. Ensuite avail. with shower/bath. Bath avail. depending on room occ. B'fast 7.30am - 9.00am, early b'fast from 7.00am by arr. Packed lunches by arr. Eve meals 6.00pm - 9.30pm. Full licence. Guest lounge. Day in OK. TV in bar. Drying facilities. Bike storage. Walkers particularly welcome. Book-ahead service.

Cheerful welcome, good food, good beer, open fire in winter, excellent value accommodation, mountains in every direction – a great place to stay. Recommended. AJ

Camusnagaul (Ross-shire)

Mrs A. Ross 4 Camusnagaul, Dundonnell by GARVE, IV23 2QT Tel: 01854 633237 STB ★★★ B&B	19 / NH 065893 Open all year. Rooms: 2T, 1D, 2F. T/F: £16.50 pp D: £18.00 pp. Single occ. T/D: any time, £none - £5.00 extra. Ensuite avail. with shower/bath. Bath avail. B'fast 8.00am - 9.00am, early b'fast from 7.00am by arr. Packed lunches by arr. Guest lounge. Day in OK. TV in guest lounge. Drying facilities. Bike storage. Book-ahead service.
Mrs Helena Ross Creaig-Ard Camusnagaul Dundonnell by GARVE, IV23 2QT Tel: 01854 633380	19 / NH 064892 Open all year. Rooms: 1D, 1F. £16.50 - £18.00 pp.* Single occ. T/D: any time, £5.00 extra. Ensuite avail. with shower. No bath. B'fast 8.30am, early b'fast any time by arr. Packed lunches by arr. Guest lounge. Day in OK. TV in guest lounge. No smoking. Drying facilities. Bike storage. Walkers particularly welcome. Book-ahead service. Children welcome, child- minding/baby-sitting by arr. *Children under 14 in family room: £12.00 pp.

Evening/bar meals:
- Dundonnell Hotel, Dundonnell, by GARVE, IV23 2QR 01854 633204   19 / NH 089881
  Bar meals 6.00pm - 8.30pm. B&B from around £55.00 pp.

Competition No. 2

To occupy yourselves while sitting in the café, watching the rain pouring down....

Name the British monarch who, during his or her reign, ascended several Munros; name the Munros which were climbed; and state the main mode of transport used up the mountains.

RULES. Please send your answers, and name and address, on a picture postcard of your home town (or your nearest locality of which picture postcards are available) to the publishers at the address on the back of the title page, by 1st July 2003. All entrants must be over 18 years of age; maximum one entry per person; no purchase necessary. In the event of any dispute, the compiler's decision is final.

PRIZES. The winner will be determined by drawing one entry out of a suitable receptacle containing all correct entries received by the closing date (or by an approximately equivalent pseudo-randomising selection process), and will be sent a bottle of single malt scotch of their choice up to a cost of £25.00. The next five correct entries drawn will each be sent a runners-up prize of a miniature of scotch whisky.

ANSWERS. The correct answers will be published on the publishers' web site after the closing date, with the names of the winner and runners-up. If no correct answers are received by the closing date, an extension period for entries may be announced on the web site.

Northern mountains (Section 16)

Strathkanaird – Knockan – Inchnadamph – Altnaharra – The Crask – Lairg

Strathkanaird *(Ross-shire)*

Alan & Chris Gibbins
Loch Dubh House, Strathkanaird
by ULLAPOOL, IV26 2TW
Tel: 01854 666224
Fax: 0870 056 9379
email: stay@lochdubhhouse.co.uk

15 / NC 147011 Open all year. Rooms: 1T, 1D, 1F. T: £18.00 - £20.00 pp D/F: £20.00 - £22.00 pp. Single occ. T/D: off peak only, no extra. Ensuite avail. with shower. Bath avail. depending on room occ. B'fast 8.30am, early b'fast from 7.00am by arr. Packed lunches by arr. Eve meal by arr. £15.00, bring your own drinks. TV in rooms. No smoking. Drying facilities. Bike storage. Walkers particularly welcome.

Fiona MacDonald
Chenoweth, 66 Strathkanaird
by ULLAPOOL, IV26 2TP
email: fiona-macdonald@
    ecosse.net
web: www.strathkanaird
    .freeserve.co.uk

15 / NC 152020 Open all year. Rooms: 2D, 1F. £20.00 - £25.00 per adult.* Single occ. T/D: any time, £5.00 - £10.00 extra. Ensuite avail. with shower. No bath. B'fast 8.00am - 9.00am, early b'fast from 7.00am by arr. Packed lunches by arr. Eve meal by arr. bring your own drinks. Guest lounge. Day in OK. TV in guest lounge. Drying facilities. Bike storage. Walkers particularly welcome. Book-ahead service. Walking Guide (a person, not a book) avail. by arr. *Prices negotiable for singles & families

Knockan *(Sutherland)*

Tom & Ray Strang
Assynt Outdoor Holidays
Birchbank Lodge, Knockan
Elphin, by LAIRG, IV27 4HH
Tel/Fax: 01854 666215
email: tomstrang@btopenworld.com
STB ★★★ Guest House
Walkers Welcome

15 / NC 213107 Open mid May - Sep. Rooms: 1S, 4T.* £21.00 pp. Single occ. T/D: if feasible, normally no extra. Ensuite avail. with shower. Bath avail. B'fast 8.30am - 9.00am, early b'fast by arr. Packed lunches by arr. Eve meal by arr. £15.00 (4 courses). Residents licence. Guest lounge. Day in OK (within reason). No TV. Drying facilities. Bike storage. Walkers particularly welcome. *Twin rooms also avail. as doubles.

Evening/bar meals:
– The Altnacealgach, by LAIRG, IV27 4HF 01854 666260   15 / NC 265109
   Bar meals all day until 9.00pm.
Teas etc:
– Elphin Tea Room, Elphin, by LAIRG, IV27 4HH 01854 666214   15 / NC 214112
   Open daily, Easter - Nov, 10.00am - 6.00pm. Homebaking, light meals.

'Bath avail.' indicates that, if desired, a bath may be taken instead of a shower, though the availability may depend on which room is occupied.

'Bath avail. depending on room occ.' indicates that the availability of a bath does depend on which room is occupied.

58

Inchnadamph (Sutherland)

Inchnadamph Hotel
Elphin, by LAIRG, IV27 4HN
Tel: 01571 822202
Fax: 01571 822203
email: inchnadamphhotel@
  fishing-scotland.co.uk
or: info@inchnadamphhotel.co.uk
web: www.inchnadamphhotel.co.uk
STB ★★★ Hotel

15 / NC 251216 Open all year. Rooms: 8S, 5T, 5D, 4F. £18.00
- £39.00 pp. Single occ. T/D: off peak only, no extra. Ensuite
avail. with shower/bath. Bath avail. B'fast 8.00am - 9.00am,
early b'fast from 7.30am by arr. Packed lunches by arr. Eve
meals: dinner 7.00pm - 8.00pm, £17.95; bar meals to 9.30pm.
Full licence. Guest lounge. Day in OK. No TV (no reception).
Drying facilities. Bike storage. Walkers particularly welcome.
Book-ahead service. Special rates DB&B for group bookings for
7 days or more, Apr, Aug, Sep, Oct.

Evening/bar meals:
– Inchnadamph Hotel *(see main entry)*
Teas etc:
– Maryck Memories of Childhood, Unapool, Kylesku, by LAIRG, IV27 4HU   15 / NC 237328
  01971 502341 Open daily, Easter - Oct, 10.00am - 5.30pm.

Altnaharra (Sutherland)

Rena & Davie Barrie
1 Macleod Crescent
Altnaharra
by LAIRG, IV27 4UG
Tel: 01549 411258

16 / NC 567352 Open Mar - Oct. Rooms: 2T, 1F. £18.00 pp.* Single occ. T/D
any time, £5.00 extra. All rooms ensuite with shower. No bath. B'fast 6.00am -
8.30am, early b'fast by arr. Packed lunches by arr. Eve meal by arr. 7.00pm,
£10.00 (3 courses), bring your own drinks. Guest lounge. Day in OK. TV in
guest lounge. Drying facilities. Bike storage. Walkers particularly welcome.
Book-ahead service. *Children under 10 in family room: £10.00 pp.

Pleasant welcome and a good breakfast. Recommended. AJ

Evening/bar meals: see also The Crask.

The Crask (Sutherland)

Mike & Kai Geldard
The Crask Inn
by LAIRG, IV27 4AB
Tel: 01549 411241
web: www.smoothhound
  .co.uk/a18821.html

16 / NC 524247 Open all year. Rooms: 2T, 1D. £20.00 pp. Single occ.
T/D: any time, no extra. Ensuite avail. with shower. Bath avail. B'fast
6.00am - 11.00am, early b'fast from 5.30am by arr. Packed lunches by arr.
Eve meals ca.7.00pm - 11.00pm, ca. £10.00 (3 courses). Full licence.
Guest lounge. Day in OK. No TV. Drying facilities. Bike storage. Book-
ahead service. 'Last Munro' celebrations a speciality. Self-catering cottage
sleeps 12, eve meals can be taken in the Inn.

*I haven't stayed here, but when I had a meal here the food came in very generous helpings. They obviously
haven't heard of 'portion control' where a measly three pieces counts as a helping of potatoes – here it was a
bowlful of over a dozen pieces. That's what you want after a day in the hills. Recommended. AJ*

*'Bath avail. all rooms' indicates that, if desired, a bath may be taken instead of a shower, and the
availability does not depend on which room is occupied, though the bath may be a shared one.*

Lairg (Sutherland)

Mr & Mrs B. Fraser
Oakhaven, Saval Road
LAIRG, IV27 4EH
Tel: 01549 402238
email: a5brf@aol.com

16 / NC 583068 Open all year, except Christmas/N.Year. Rooms: 1S, 1T, 1D. S: £15.00 - £17.00 pp T/D: £16.00 pp. Single occ. T/D any time, £none - £3.00 extra. No ensuite. Bath avail. B'fast 7.00am - 9.00am, early b'fast from 5.30am by arr. Packed lunches by arr. Guest lounge. Day in OK. TV in guest lounge. Drying facilities. Bike storage. Book-ahead service.

Margaret & David Walker
Park House, Station Road
LAIRG, IV27 4AU
Tel: 01549 402208 Fax: 01549 402693
email: dwalker@
park-house30.freeserve.co.uk
web: www.fishinscotland.net/parkhouse
STB ★★★ B&B, Walkers Welcome

16 / NC 582062 Open all year, except Christmas/N.Year. Rooms: 2T, 1D. £23.00 - £27.00 pp. Single occ. T/D: any time, £5.00 - £12.00 extra. Ensuite avail. with shower/bath. Bath avail. depending on room occ. B'fast 8.00am - 9.00am, early b'fast from 7.30am by arr. Packed lunches by arr. Eve meal by arr. 7.30pm - 8.00pm, £16.00. Residents licence. Guest lounge. Day in OK. TV in rooms. Drying facilities. Bike storage. Book-ahead service.

Mrs B. M. Paterson
Strathwin, Ferry Croft
LAIRG, IV27 4AZ
Tel: 01549 402487

16 / NC 580061 Open Apr - Sep. Rooms: 1T, 1D. £15.00 pp. Single occ. T/D any time, no extra. No ensuite. Bath avail. B'fast 8.00am - 8.30am, early b'fast from 6.00am by arr. Guest lounge. Day in OK. TV in rooms & guest lounge. Drying facilities. Bike storage. Book-ahead service.

Mrs K. Fraser
Kincora, Lochside
LAIRG, IV27 4EG
Tel: 01549 402062

16 / NC 580069 Open Mar - Nov. Rooms: 2D. £16.00 pp. Single occ. T/D: off peak only, £4.00 extra. No ensuite. Bath avail. B'fast 8.30am, early b'fast by arr. Packed lunches by arr. Guest lounge. TV in guest lounge. Drying facilities. Bike storage. Book-ahead service. Light supper each evening at no extra cost.

George & Lorna Morgan
Lochview, Lochside
LAIRG, IV27 4EH
Tel/Fax: 01549 402578
STB Awaiting
Inspection

16 / NC 582067 Open all year. Rooms: 2T, 1D. £18.00 pp. Single occ. T/D: any time, £2.00 extra. All rooms ensuite with shower. Bath avail. B'fast 7.30am - 8.45am, early b'fast from 6.00am by arr. Packed lunches by arr. Eve meal by arr. 6.00pm - 8.00pm, £8.50, bring your own drinks. Guest lounge. Day in OK. TV in rooms & guest lounge. No smoking. Drying facilities. Bike storage. Walkers particularly welcome. Book-ahead service. Hillwalking proprietors.

Evening/bar meals:
- The Nip Inn, Main Street, LAIRG, IV27 4DB 01549 402243   16 / NC 584063
  info@nipinn.co.uk Bar meals 6.00pm - 9.00pm. B&B from around £27.00 pp.
Tourist info: Ferrycroft Centre, LAIRG, IV27 4AZ 01549 402160 (Apr - Oct)

Isle of Mull & Isle of Skye (Section 17)

Gruline – Salen – Craignure – Broadford – Ard Dorch – Sconser – Drynoch – Carbost

Gruline, Mull (Argyll)

Sue & John Bebbington
Barn Cottage & Stables, Gruline
ISLE OF MULL, PA71 6HR
Tel: 01680 300451
email: bebbington@
    barncottagemull.freeserve.co.uk
web: www.webscot.com/barncottage
STB ★★★ B&B

48 / NM 548399 Open all year. Rooms: 1T, 1F. £18.00 pp.*
Single occ. T/D: any time, £2.00 extra. No ensuite. Bath avail.
B'fast any time - 9.00am by arr. Packed lunches by arr. Eve
meal by arr. off peak season only. Guest lounge. Day in OK.
TV in guest lounge. No smoking. Drying facilities. Bike
storage. Book-ahead service. Walking books, guides & maps
avail. *Children 5 - 11 in family room: half price.

Evening/bar meals: see Salen

Salen, Mull (Argyll)

Eilidh Allan
Aros View, Salen, Aros
ISLE OF MULL, PA72 6JB
Tel: 01680 300372
email: arosview@supanet.com
www.arosview.plus.com
STB ★★★ B&B
Friendly welcome and a good breakfast. Recommended. AJ

48 / NM 574430 Open all year. Rooms: 1T, 1D. £18.50 pp. Single
occ. T/D: any time, £5.00 extra. Ensuite avail. with shower/bath.
Bath avail. depending on room occ. B'fast 7.30am - 8.30am, early
b'fast any time by arr. Packed lunches by arr. Eve meal by arr.
7.00pm, £7.50, bring your own drinks. Day in room OK. TV in rooms.
No smoking. Drying facilities. Bike storage. Book-ahead service.

Martin & Judith Keivers
Fascadail, Salen, Aros
ISLE OF MULL, PA72 6JB
Tel: 01680 300444
email: keivers@tesco.net
web: www.zynet.co.uk/mull/fascadail
STB ★★★ B&B

48 / NM 574430   Open all year.   Rooms: 1T, 2D.   From
£20.00 pp. Single occ. T/D: any time, £5.00 - £20.00 extra. All
rooms ensuite with shower. No bath. B'fast 7.30am - 8.30am,
early b'fast by arr. Packed lunches by arr. Day in room OK. TV
in rooms. No smoking. Drying facilities. Bike storage. Walkers
particularly welcome. Book-ahead service.

Dave & Teresa Mountifield
Rock Cottage, Salen, Aros
ISLE OF MULL, PA72 6JB
Tel: 01680 300506
Mob: 07971 191728
email: rockcottage@mull.com
web: www.rockcottage.mull.com
STB ★★★ B&B, Walkers Welcome

48 / NM 581429 Open all year. Rooms: 1T. £18.50 pp. Single
occ. T/D: any time, no extra. Ensuite avail. with shower. No bath.
B'fast 8.00am - 9.30am, early b'fast from 6.30am by arr. Packed
lunches by arr. Day in room OK. TV in room. No smoking.
Drying facilities. Bike storage. Walkers particularly welcome.
Book-ahead service. Self catering caravan avail. Pick up from
ferry terminal by arr. Drop off & pick up service around island
during stay.

Please read the entries in conjunction with the notes on pages 5 & 6.

Mrs Linda Crossley
Dunvegan Cottage, Pier Road, Salen
Aros, ISLE OF MULL, PA72 6JL
Tel: 01680 300387 Mob: 07773 951401
email: linda@crossley.abel.co.uk
web: www.welcome.to/dunvegancottage
or: www.electricscotland.com/accom/dunvegan
STB ★★ B&B

48 / NM 575432 Open all year. Rooms: 2F.
£15.00 pp. Single occ. T/D: off peak only,
£10.00 extra. No ensuite. Bath avail. B'fast
7.00am - 9.00am, early b'fast by arr. Packed
lunches by arr. Guest lounge. Day in OK. TV
in guest lounge. No smoking. Drying facilities.
Bike storage. Book-ahead service.

Carol & Clifford Pauley
Tigh-an-Achadh
Salen, Aros
ISLE OF MULL
PA72 6JF
Tel: 01680 300669

48 / NM 572429 Open all year. Rooms: 1D, 1F. £20.00 - £24.00 pp.* Single
occ. T/D: off peak only, £3.00 extra. Ensuite avail. with bath & shower
attachment. Bath avail. both rooms. B'fast 8.00am - 9.30am, early b'fast by
arr. Packed lunches by arr. Eve meal by arr. Lounge shared with hosts. Day
in room OK. TV in rooms. No smoking. Drying facilities. Bike storage.
*Children under 11 in family room: half price.

Evening/bar meals:
– The Salen Hotel, Salen, Aros, ISLE OF MULL, PA72 6JE 01680 300324   48 / NM 573431
  salenhotelmull@barbox.net Bar meals 6.00pm - 8.30pm. B&B from around £27.00 pp.
Teas etc:
– The Coffee Pot, Salen, Aros, ISLE OF MULL, PA72 6JG 01680 300555   48 / NM 572431
  Open daily, Easter - mid Oct, 9.30am - 5.00pm (Mon - Sat), 11.00am - 5.00pm (Sun);
  open 6.00pm - 8.00pm (May - Sep) for pizzas & pasta dishes by reservation.

Craignure, Mull (Argyll)

Mrs M. MacLachlan
Aon a' Dha, Kirk Terrace, Craignure
ISLE OF MULL, PA65 6AZ
Tel: 01680 812318
STB ★★ B&B

49 / NM 721366 Open all year, except Christmas/N.Year. Rooms:
1T, 2D. £16.00 pp (room only £11.00 pp). Single occ. T/D: any
time, no extra. No ensuite. Bath avail. B'fast 7.30am - 8.30am,
early b'fast from 7.00am by arr. Guest lounge. Day in OK. TV in
guest lounge. Drying facilities. Bike storage. Book-ahead service.

Evening/bar meals:
– Craignure Inn, Craignure, ISLE OF MULL, PA65 6AY 01680 812305   49 / NM 720368
  www.craignure-inn.co.uk Bar meals 5.00pm - 8.30pm. B&B from around £35.00 pp.
Tourist info: The Pier, Craignure, ISLE OF MULL, PA65 6AY 01680 812377 (All year)

Broadford, Skye (Ross-shire)

Mrs Dolina Robertson
Westside, Torrin Road, Broadford
ISLE OF SKYE, IV49 9AB
Tel/Fax: 01471 822320
email: dolly.skye@talk21.com
web: www.isleofskye.net/westside
STB ★★★★ B&B

32 / NG 639234 Open Feb - mid Dec. Rooms: 1S, 1T, 1D.
£22.00 pp. Single occ. T/D: off peak only, £5.00 extra. Ensuite
avail. with shower/bath. Bath avail. depending on room occ.
B'fast 8.30am, early b'fast from 7.00am by arr. Guest lounge.
Day in OK. TV in rooms & guest lounge. No smoking. Drying
facilities. Walkers particularly welcome. Book-ahead service.

Isle of Mull & Isle of Skye (Section 17)

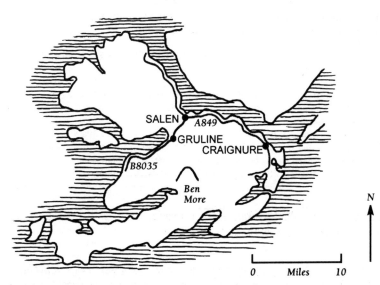

Locations in CAPITALS have listed accommodation

Philip & Viera Tordoff Millbrae Lower Harrapool Broadford ISLE OF SKYE, IV49 9AE Tel/Fax: 01471 822310	32 / NG 649230 Open Mar - late Oct. Rooms: 1S, 1T, 2D. S: £18.00 - £22.00 pp T/D: £16.00 - £22.00 pp. Single occ. T/D: off peak only, £5.00 extra. All rooms ensuite with shower. No bath. B'fast 8.00am - 8.45am, early b'fast from 7.30am by arr. Packed lunches by arr. Guest lounge. Day in OK. TV in guest lounge. No smoking. Drying facilities. Bike storage. Walkers particularly welcome. Book-ahead service. Transport to drop off walkers may be avail. Proprietors are members of the John Muir Trust.
Mrs M. Mackenzie Caberfeidh 1 Harrapool, Broadford ISLE OF SKYE, IV49 9AQ Tel: 01471 822664 STB ★★★ B&B	32 / NG 649232 Open all year, except Christmas/N.Year. Rooms: 3D. £18.00 - £23.00 pp. Single occ. T/D: off peak only, £10.00 extra. Ensuite avail. with shower. Bath avail. B'fast 7.30am - 8.45am, early b'fast from 7.00am by arr. Packed lunches by arr. Guest lounge. Day in OK. TV in rooms & guest lounge. No smoking. Drying facilities. Walkers particularly welcome. Book-ahead service.
Alex & Catherine Shearer The Shieling Lower Harrapool Broadford, ISLE OF SKYE IV49 9AE Tel: 01471 822533	32 / NG 649231 Open all year, except Christmas/N.Year. Rooms: 1S, 1T, 1D, 1F. S: £16.00 - £22.00 pp T: £15.00 - £22.00 pp D: £14.00 - £18.00 pp F: £15.00 - £18.00 per adult.* Single occ. T/D: off peak only, £varies extra. Ensuite avail. with shower. Bath avail. depending on room occ. B'fast 7.30am - 8.30am. Guest lounge. TV in rooms. No smoking. Bike storage. Book-ahead service. *Children under 11 in family room: reduced rate. Proprietors also own the Skye Serpentarium – good for a wet day.

Evening/bar meals: *Skye*   01478 650204
- Broadford Hotel, Broadford, ISLE OF SKYE, IV49 9AB 01471 822204   32 / NG 640235
  Bar meals 6.00pm - 8.30pm. B&B from around £33.00 pp.
- Dunollie Hotel, Broadford, ISLE OF SKYE, IV49 9AE 01471 822253   32 / NG 645234
  Bar meals 6.00pm - 9.00pm. B&B from around £30.00 pp.
Teas etc:
- The Fig Tree Tea Room & Restaurant, Broadford, ISLE OF SKYE, IV49 9AB   32 / NG 638237
  01471 822616 Open daily, Easter - Sep, 10.30am - 9.00pm.
Bike hire:
- Sutherlands Garage, Broadford, ISLE OF SKYE, IV49 9AB 01471 822225
Tourist info: The Car Park, Broadford, ISLE OF SKYE, IV49 9AB 01471 822361 (Apr - Oct)
Ferry service, Elgol – Loch Coruisk:
- *'Bella Jane'*, Donald & Bella MacKinnon, Tel: 01471 866244 (7.30am - 10.00am).
  Runs 1st Apr - mid Oct, £12.00 single, booking essential. Charter also available.
  web: www.bellajane.co.uk Second boat due to enter service late summer 2002,
  allowing more flexibility for places to land. See www.aquaxplore.co.uk.

'No smoking' means that smoking is totally banned, if not stated, assume that it is restricted, and check with the proprietors if you wish to smoke.

'Day in OK' means that you may stay in your room (or guest lounge, if available) during the day, but this does not apply on your day of arrival or departure, and access to service the room must be allowed at some time.

Ard Dorch, Skye (Ross-shire)

Gill & Steve Terry
The Skye Picture House, Ard Dorch
Broadford, ISLE OF SKYE, IV49 9AJ
Tel: 01471 822531 Fax: 01471 822305
email: gill@skyepicturehouse.co.uk
web: www.skyepicturehouse.co.uk
STB ★★★ Guest House
Walkers Welcome

32 / NG 582285 Open all year. Rooms: 2S, 1T, 2D, 1F. £18.00 - £26.00 pp.*   Single occ. T/D: any time, £none - £varies. Ensuite avail. with shower/bath. Bath avail. B'fast 8.00am - 9.00am, early b'fast from 7.00am by arr. Packed lunches by arr. Eve meal by arr. 7.00pm, £12.00. Residents licence. Guest lounge. Day in OK. TV in guest lounge. No smoking. Drying facilities. Bike storage. Walkers particularly welcome. Book-ahead service. *Reduced rates for children in family room.

Evening/bar meals: see also Broadford

Sconser, Skye (Ross-shire)

Mrs M. Jagger
Loch Aluinn, 7 Sconser
ISLE OF SKYE, IV48 8TD
Tel: 01478 650288
email: loch-aluinn@
        lineone.net
STB ★★★★ B&B

32 / NG 515317 Open Mar - Oct. Rooms: 1T, 1D. £23.00 - £24.00 pp. No single occ. T/D. Ensuite avail. with shower/bath. Bath avail. depending on room occ. B'fast 8.00am - 8.30am, early b'fast from 7.30am by arr. Packed lunches by arr. Eve meal by arr. 7.00pm - 8.00pm, £14.00 (3 courses), bring your own drinks. Guest lounge. Day in OK. TV in rooms & guest lounge. No smoking. Book-ahead service. Maps & walking guides avail. for day loan. Self-catering unit avail.

Chrissie & Hector MacLeod
The Old Schoolhouse, Sconser
ISLE OF SKYE, IV48 8TD
Tel/Fax: 01478 650313
Mob: 07714 653394
email: hectormacld@aol.com

32 / NG 523320 Open Mar - Nov. Rooms: 1T, 1D, 1F. £15.00 - £16.00 pp. No single occ. T/D. No ensuite. Bath avail. all rooms. B'fast 8.00am - 8.30am, early b'fast by arr. Packed lunches by arr. Day in room OK. TV in rooms. No smoking. Drying facilities. Bike storage. Book-ahead service.

Evening/bar meals:
- Sligachan Hotel, Sligachan, Carbost, ISLE OF SKYE, IV47 8SW   32 / NG 485298
  01478 650204 reservations@sligachan.co.uk www.sligachan.co.uk
  Bar meals 6.00pm - 9.00pm. B&B from around £40.00 pp.
- Sconser Lodge Hotel, Sconser, ISLE OF SKYE, IV48 8TD 01478 650333   32 / NG 532322
  Bar meals 6.00pm - 8.30pm. B&B from around £35.00 pp.

Drynoch, Skye (Ross-shire)

Mrs Donna Campbell
Drynoch Farm House, Drynoch
Carbost, ISLE OF SKYE, IV47 8SX
Tel/Fax: 01478 640441
Mob: 07901 778342
email: donnadrynoch@yahoo.co.uk
or: donnadrynoch@hotmail.com
web: www.isleofskye.net/drynochhouse
STB ★★ B&B

32 / NG 402316 Open all year. Rooms: 1S, 2F. £17.00 - £18.00 pp. Single occ. T/D: off peak only, no extra. No ensuite. Bath avail. B'fast 8.00am - 9.00am, early b'fast by arr. Packed lunches by arr. Eve meal by arr. £10.00 (2 courses) - £12.50 (3 courses), bring your own drinks. Guest lounge. Day in OK. TV in guest lounge. No smoking. Drying facilities. Bike storage. Walkers particularly welcome. Book-ahead service. Pick-up service from bus at Sligachan.

I haven't stayed here, but the welcome I received when I called in means I would very much like to. Recommended. AJ.

Evening/bar meals: see also Carbost

Carbost, Skye (Ross-shire)

The Old Inn
Carbost
ISLE OF SKYE
IV47 8SR
Tel/Fax: 01478 640205
email: oldinn@
    carbost.f9.co.uk
web: www.carbost.f9.co.uk
STB ★ Inn

32 / NG 380317 Open all year. Rooms: 1S, 2T, 2D, 1F. S/T/D: £26.50 pp F: £82.00 per room (2 adults + 2 children). Single occ. T/D: any time, £9.50 extra. Ensuite avail. with shower/bath. Bath avail. depending on room occ. B'fast 8.00am - 9.30am, early b'fast from 7.30am by arr. Packed lunches by arr. Eve meals 6.00pm - 9.00pm. Full licence. Day in room OK. TV in rooms. Drying facilities. Bike storage. Walkers particularly welcome. Book-ahead service. Reductions for longer stays. Bunkhouse avail. £10.00 - £12.00 pp with kitchen, common room (with TV), drying room, washing facilities – good for groups.

I haven't stayed here, but I've had several first-rate meals here. Recommended for food. AJ

Murray & Norma Campbell
Langal, 9 Carbostmor
Carbost, ISLE OF SKYE, IV47 8ST
Tel: 01478 640409
email: murray@campb2.fsnet.co.uk
web: www.visitscotland.com
    /accommodation/index.asp
STB ★★★ B&B

32 / NG 386312 Open all year. Rooms: 1T, 2D. T: £17.00 pp D: £17.00/£22.00 pp. Single occ. T/D: any time, £none - £5.00 extra. Ensuite avail. with shower. Bath avail. B'fast 7.30am - 8.30am, early b'fast from 6.30am by arr. Packed lunches by arr. Guest lounge. Day in OK. TV in rooms. No smoking. Drying facilities. Bike storage. Walkers particularly welcome. Book-ahead service.

Evening/bar meals:
  – The Old Inn *(see main entry)*
Bike hire:
  – Carbost Mountain Bike Hire, 5 Carbostbeg, Carbost, ISLE OF SKYE, IV47 8SH
    01478 640247

Index